Lectionary
Advent 2023 to the eve of Advent 2024 (Year B)

Church House Publishing

Published by	Church House Publishing Church House Great Smith Street London SW1P 3AZ
Compilation ©	*The Archbishops' Council 2023*
ISBN	978-0-7151-2413-0 Standard 978-0-7151-2414-7 Large 978-0-7151-2415-4 eBook

Authorization	The Common Worship Calendar and Lectionaries are authorized pursuant to Canon B 2 of the Canons of the Church of England for use until further resolution of the General Synod of the Church of England.

Copyright and Acknowledgements	The Revised Common Lectionary is copyright © The Consultation on Common Texts: 1992. The Church of England adaptations to the Principal Service Lectionary are copyright © The Archbishops' Council, as are the Second and Third Service Lectionaries, the Weekday Lectionary for Morning and Evening Prayer and the Additional Weekday Lectionary. The Daily Eucharistic Lectionary derives, with some adaptation, from the Ordo Lectionum Missae of the Roman Catholic Church and is reproduced by permission of The International Commission on English in the Liturgy. Edited by Peter Moger Designed by Derek Birdsall & John Morgan/Omnific Typeset by RefineCatch Ltd, Bungay, Suffolk Printed in England by Core Publications Ltd

Contents of this booklet

This booklet gives details of the full range of possibilities envisaged in the liturgical calendar and lectionary of Common Worship. Its use as a tool for the preparation of worship will require the making of several choices based first on the general celebration of the Christian year by the Church of England as a whole; second on the customary pattern of calendar in the diocese, parish and place of worship; and third on the pattern of services locally.

The **first column** comprises the Calendar of the Church with the days of the year. Observances that are mandatory are printed either in **bold** type (Sundays), in **bold** type (Principal Feasts and Holy Days) or in roman (Festivals). Optional celebrations (Lesser Festivals) and Commemorations are printed in ordinary roman type and *italic* type respectively.

The **second column** comprises (a) the readings and psalms for the Principal Service on Sundays, Principal Feasts and Holy Days, and Festivals, and (b) Holy Communion readings and psalms for other days of the week. On the Sundays after Trinity, the Old Testament reading and its psalm are divided into two smaller columns, indicating a choice between a 'continuous' reading week by week or a reading 'related' to the Gospel for that day.

The **third column** comprises (a) the Third Service readings and psalms for Sundays, Principal Feasts and Holy Days, and Festivals, and (b) the readings and psalms for weekday Morning Prayer.

The **fourth column** comprises (a) the Second Service readings and psalms for Sundays, Principal Feasts and Holy Days, and Festivals, and (b) the readings and psalms for weekday Evening Prayer.

An **Additional Weekday Lectionary**, intended particularly for use in places of worship that attract occasional rather than daily worshippers, is provided on pages 70–77. It may be used either at Morning or Evening Prayer.

Common of the Saints

General readings and psalms for saints' days can be found on pages 79–83; for some particular celebrations, other readings are suggested there.

Special Occasions

Readings and psalms for special occasions can be found on pages 84–85.

Liturgical colours

Appropriate liturgical colours are suggested in this booklet. They are not mandatory; traditional or local use may be followed.

Colours are indicated by single letters: the first (always upper case) for the season or Festival; and occasionally a second (lower case) for an optional celebration on that day. Thus, for example, Gr for the celebration of a Lesser Festival whose liturgical colour is red, in an otherwise 'green' season.

The following abbreviations are used:

G	Green
P or p	Purple or Violet
P(La)	Purple or Lent array
R or r	Red
W or w	White (Gold is indicated where its use would be appropriate)

Notes on the Lectionary

Sundays, Principal Feasts and Holy Days and Festivals

Three sets of psalms and readings are provided for each Sunday, Principal Feast or Holy Day and Festival.

The **Principal Service lectionary** (based on the Revised Common Lectionary) is intended for use at the principal service of the day (whether this service is Holy Communion or some other authorized form). In most Church communities, this is likely to be the mid-morning service, but the minister is free to decide which service time normally constitutes the Principal Service of the day. This lectionary may be used twice if required – for example, at an early celebration of Holy Communion and then again at a later one.

If only **two readings** are used at the Principal Service and that service is Holy Communion, the second reading must always be the Gospel reading. When the Principal Service lectionary is used at a service other than Holy Communion, the Gospel reading need not always be chosen.

The **Second Service lectionary** is intended for a second main service. In many churches, this lectionary may be the appropriate provision for a Sunday afternoon or evening service. A Gospel reading is always provided so that this lectionary can, if necessary, be used where the second main service is a celebration of Holy Communion.

The **Third Service lectionary**, with shorter readings, is intended where a third set of psalms and readings is needed and is most appropriate for use at an office. A Gospel reading is not always provided, so this lectionary is not suitable for use at Holy Communion.

Weekdays

The Common Worship Weekday Lectionary authorized by the General Synod in 2005 comprises a lectionary (with psalms) for Holy Communion, a lectionary for Morning and Evening Prayer, and tables of psalms for Morning and Evening Prayer.

The **Daily Eucharistic Lectionary** (based on the Roman Catholic daily eucharistic lectionary) is a semi-continuous two-year lectionary with a wide use of scripture, though not complete coverage of the Bible. Two readings are provided for each day, the first from either the Old or New Testament, the second always a Gospel. Psalm provision is intended to be a brief response to the first reading. It is for use at Holy Communion normally in places with a daily or near-daily celebration with a regular congregation. It may also be used as an office lectionary.

The **lectionary for Morning and Evening Prayer** always provides two readings for each office, the first from the Old Testament and the second from the New Testament. These are generally in sequence. One of the New Testament readings for any particular day is from the Gospels.

The **psalms for Morning and Evening Prayer** follow a sequential pattern in Ordinary Time (apart from the period from All Saints to the beginning of Advent).

In the periods from All Saints until 18 December, from the Epiphany until the Presentation of Christ in the Temple (Candlemas), from Ash Wednesday until Palm Sunday, and from the Monday after Easter Week until Pentecost, there is a choice of psalms at Morning and Evening Prayer. The psalms printed first reflect the theme of the season. Alternatively, the psalms from the Ordinary Time cycle may be used. The two sets are separated by 'or'.

From 19 December until the Epiphany and from the Monday of Holy Week until the Saturday of Easter Week, only seasonal psalms are provided.

Where more than one psalm is given, one psalm (printed in **bold**) may be used as the sole psalm at that office.

Guidance on how these options for saying the psalms are expressed typographically can be found in the 'Notes on the Lectionary' below.

A further cycle is provided (see table on page 86), which is largely the monthly sequential cycle of psalms given in the *Book of Common Prayer*.

A single psalm for use by those who only say one office each day is provided in Prayer During the Day in *Common Worship: Daily Prayer*.

An **Additional Weekday Lectionary**, intended particularly for use in places of worship that attract occasional rather than daily worshippers, is provided on pages 70–77. It can be used either at Morning or Evening Prayer. Psalmody is not provided and should be taken from provision outlined above.

Using the Lectionary tables

All **Bible references** (except to the Psalms) are to the *New Revised Standard Version* (New York, 1989). Those who use other Bible translations should check the verse numbers against the *NRSV*. Each reference gives book, chapter and verse, in that order.

References to the Psalms are to the Common Worship psalter, published in *Common Worship: Services and Prayers for the Church of England* (2000) and *Common Worship: Daily Prayer* (2005). A table showing the verse number differences between this and the psalter in the *Book of Common Prayer* is provided on the Church of England website (https://www.churchofengland.org/prayer-and-worship/worship-texts-and-resources/common-worship/daily-prayer/psalter/psalter-verse).

Options in the provision of readings or psalms are presented in the following ways:

¶ square brackets [xx] give either optional additional verses or Psalms, or a shorter alternative;
¶ 'or' indicates a simple choice between two alternative readings or courses of psalms;
¶ a psalm printed in **bold** may be used as the sole psalm at that office;
¶ on weekdays a psalm printed in parentheses (xx) is omitted if it has been used as the opening canticle at that office;
¶ a psalm marked with an asterisk may be shortened if desired.

Where a reading from the **Apocrypha** is offered, an alternative Old Testament reading is provided.

In the choice of **readings other than the Gospel** reading, the minister should ensure that, in any year, a balance is maintained between readings from the Old and New Testaments and that, where a particular biblical book is appointed to be read over several weeks, the choice ensures that the continuity of one book is not lost.

On the Sundays after Trinity, the Principal Service Lectionary provides **alternative Old Testament readings and psalms**. References in the left-hand column (under the heading 'Continuous') offer a *semi-continuous* reading of Old Testament texts. Such a reading and its complementary psalmody stand independently of the other readings. References in the right-hand column (under the heading 'Related') *relate* the Old Testament reading and the psalm to the Gospel reading. One column should be followed for the whole sequence of Sundays after Trinity.

The Lectionary 2023–2024

The Sunday and festal readings for 3 December 2023 (the First Sunday of Advent) to 30 November 2024 (the eve of Advent Sunday) are from **Year B**, which offers a semi-continuous reading of Mark's Gospel at the Principal Service on Sundays throughout the year.

The weekday readings for Holy Communion are from **Year Two** of the Daily Eucharistic Lectionary (DEL).

Office readings are from Table 1 of the Weekday Lectionary: at Morning Prayer, Old Testament 1 and New Testament 1; and, at Evening Prayer, Old Testament 2b in Ordinary Time and 2a in Seasonal Time, and New Testament 2.

Notes on the Calendar 27 December 2023— 30 November 2024

These notes are based on the Rules to Order the Christian Year (*Common Worship: Times and Seasons*, pages 24–30).

Sundays

All Sundays celebrate the paschal mystery of the death and resurrection of the Lord. They also reflect the character of the seasons in which they are set.

Principal Feasts

On these days (printed in bold) Holy Communion is celebrated in every cathedral and in at least one church in each benefice or, where benefices are held in plurality, in at least one church in at least one of those benefices, and this celebration, required by Canon B 14, may not be displaced by any other celebration, and may be dispensed with only in accordance with the provision of Canon B 14A.

Except in the case of Christmas Day and Easter Day, the celebration of the Feast *begins with Evening Prayer on the day before the Feast*, and the Collect at that Evening Prayer is that of the Feast. In the case of Christmas Eve and Easter Eve, there is proper liturgical provision (including a Collect) for the whole day.

The Epiphany may, for pastoral reasons, be celebrated on Sunday 7 January. **The Presentation of Christ in the Temple** (Candlemas) is celebrated either on Friday 2 February or on Sunday 28 January. **All Saints' Day** may be celebrated on Sunday 3 November (replacing the Fourth Sunday before Advent), with or without a supplementary celebration on Friday 1 November.

Other Principal Holy Days

These days (printed in bold), and the liturgical provision for them, may not be displaced by any other celebration.

Ash Wednesday (14 February) and **Maundy Thursday** (28 March) are Principal Holy Days. On both these days Holy Communion is celebrated in every cathedral and in at least one church in each benefice or, where benefices are held in plurality, in at least one church in at least one of those benefices, except where there is dispensation under Canon B 14A.

Good Friday (29 March) is a Principal Holy Day.

Eastertide

The paschal character of **the Great Fifty Days of Easter**, from Easter Day (31 March) to Pentecost (19 May), should be celebrated throughout the season, and should not be displaced by other celebrations. No Festival day may be celebrated in Easter Week; and nor may any Festival – except for a Patronal or Dedication Festival – displace the celebration of a Sunday (a memorial of the resurrection) during Eastertide. The paschal character of the season should be retained on those weekdays when saints' days are celebrated.

The three days before Ascension Day (6–8 May) are customarily observed as **Rogation Days**, when prayer is offered for God's blessing on the fruits of the earth and on human labour.

The nine days **after Ascension Day until the eve of Pentecost** (10–18 May) are observed as days of prayer and preparation for the celebration of the outpouring of the Holy Spirit.

Ordinary Time

Ordinary Time comprises two periods in the year: first, the period from the day after the Presentation of Christ in the Temple until the day before Ash Wednesday, and second, that from the day after Pentecost until the day before the First Sunday of Advent.

During Ordinary Time, there is no seasonal emphasis, except that the period between All Saints' Day and the First Sunday of Advent is a time to celebrate and reflect upon the reign of Christ in earth and heaven.

Festivals

These days (printed in roman), and the liturgical provision for them, are not usually displaced. For each day there is full liturgical provision for a Principal, Second and Third Service, and an optional so-called First Evening Prayer on the evening before the Festival where this is required.

Festivals may *not* be celebrated on Sundays in Advent, Lent or Eastertide, the Baptism of Christ, Ascension Day, Trinity Sunday or Christ the King, or weekdays between Palm Sunday and the Second Sunday of Easter.

Otherwise, Festivals falling on a Sunday – namely in 2023–24, Michael and All Angels (falling on the Eighteenth Sunday after Trinity) – may be kept on that Sunday or transferred to the Monday (or, at the discretion of the minister, to the next suitable weekday).

Certain Festivals (namely, Matthias the Apostle, the Visit of the Blessed Virgin Mary to Elizabeth, Thomas the Apostle, and the Blessed Virgin Mary) have customary alternative dates (see p.8).

The Thursday after Trinity Sunday (30 May) may be observed as the **Day of Thanksgiving for the Institution of Holy Communion** (sometimes known as *Corpus Christi*), and may be kept as a Festival.

Other Celebrations

Mothering Sunday falls on the Fourth Sunday of Lent (10 March). Alternative prayers and readings are provided for the Principal Service. **Bible Sunday** may be celebrated on 27 October, replacing the Last Sunday after Trinity, and appropriate prayers and readings are provided.

Local Celebrations

The celebration of **the patron saint or the title of a church** is kept either as a Festival or as a Principal Feast.

The **Dedication Festival** of a church is the anniversary of the date of its dedication or consecration. This is kept either as a Festival or as a Principal Feast. When kept as Principal Feasts, the Patronal and Dedication Festivals may be transferred to the nearest Sunday, unless that day is already a Principal Feast or one of the following days: the First Sunday of Advent, the Baptism of Christ, the First Sunday of Lent, the Fifth Sunday of Lent, or Palm Sunday. If the actual date is not known, the Dedication Festival may be celebrated on 6 October (replacing the Nineteenth Sunday after Trinity), or on 27 October (replacing the Last Sunday after Trinity), or on a suitable date chosen locally. Readings can be found on page 78.

Harvest Thanksgiving may be celebrated on any Sunday in autumn, replacing the provision for that day, provided it does not displace any Principal Feast or Festival.

Diocesan and other local provision may be made in **the calendar of the saints** to supplement the general calendar, in accordance with Canon B 6, paragraph 5.

Lesser Festivals

Lesser Festivals (printed in ordinary roman type, in black) are observed in a manner appropriate to a particular place. Each is provided with a Collect, which may supersede the Collect of the week. For certain Lesser Festivals a complete set of Eucharistic readings is provided, and for others appropriate readings may be selected from the Common of the Saints (see pages 79–83). These readings may, at the minister's discretion, supersede the Daily Eucharistic Lectionary (DEL). The weekday psalms and readings at Morning and Evening Prayer are not usually superseded by those for Lesser Festivals, but at the minister's discretion psalms and readings provided on these days for use at Holy Communion may be used instead at Morning or Evening Prayer.

The minister may be selective in the Lesser Festivals that are observed and may also keep some, or all of them, as Commemorations, perhaps especially in Advent, Lent and Easter where the character of the season ought to be sustained. If the Day of Thanksgiving for the Institution of Holy Communion (30 May) is not kept as a Festival in 2024, it may be kept as a Lesser Festival.

When a Lesser Festival falls on a Principal Feast or Holy Day, a Festival, a Sunday, or on a weekday between Palm Sunday and the Second Sunday of Easter, its celebration is normally omitted for that year. However, where there is sufficient reason, it may, at the discretion of the minister, be celebrated on the nearest available day.

Commemorations

Commemorations (printed in *italic*) are made by a mention in prayers of intercession. They are not provided with Collect, Psalm and Readings, and do not replace the usual weekday provision at Holy Communion or at Morning and Evening Prayer.

The minister may be selective in the Commemorations that are made.

Only where there is an established celebration in the wider Church or where the day has a special local significance may a Commemoration be observed as a Lesser Festival, with liturgical provision from the Common of the Saints (pages 79–83).

In designating a Commemoration as a Lesser Festival, the minister must remember the need to maintain the spirit of the season, especially of Advent, Lent and Easter.

Days of Discipline and Self-Denial

The weekdays of Lent and every Friday in the year are days of discipline and self-denial, with the exception of Principal Feasts, Festivals outside Lent, and Fridays from Easter Day to Pentecost. The day preceding a Principal Feast may also be appropriately kept as a day of discipline and self-denial in preparation for the Feast.

Ember Days

Ember Days should be kept, under the bishop's directions, in the week before an ordination as days of prayer for those to be ordained deacon or priest.

Ember Days may also be kept even when there is no ordination in the diocese as more general days of prayer for those who serve the Church in its various ministries, both ordained and lay, and for vocations. Traditionally they have been observed on the Wednesday, Friday and Saturday in the week before the Third Sunday of Advent, the Second Sunday of Lent, and the Sundays nearest to 29 June and 29 September.

Notes on Collects

For a table showing where the Collects and Post Communions are published, see page 78.

Where a Collect ends 'through Jesus Christ … now and for ever', the minister may omit the longer (trinitarian) ending and use the shorter ending, 'through Jesus Christ our Lord', to which the people respond, 'Amen'. The longer ending, however, is to be preferred at a service of Holy Communion.

The Collect for each Sunday is used at Evening Prayer on the Saturday preceding, except where that Saturday is a Principal Feast, or a Festival, or the eve of Christmas Day or Easter Day. The Collect for each Sunday is also used on the weekdays following, except where other provision is made.

Abbreviations used in this book

Alt	Alternative
BVM	Blessed Virgin Mary
DEL	Daily Eucharistic Lectionary
EP	Evening Prayer
G	Green

| HC | Holy Communion: used where additional references are given to provide alternative texts for use at a celebration of Holy Communion (most often the provision of a psalm or gospel) |
| MP | Morning Prayer |

P or p	Purple or Violet
P(La)	Purple or Lent Array
Ps & Pss	Psalmody
R or r	Red
W or w	White (Gold is indicated where its use would be appropriate)

Alternative dates

The following may be celebrated on the alternative dates indicated:

Chad
– with Cedd on 26 October instead of 2 March

Cuthbert
– on 4 September instead of 20 March

Thomas the Apostle
– on 21 December 2023 instead of 3 July 2024

Matthias the Apostle
– on 24 February instead of 14 May

The Visit of the Blessed Virgin Mary to Elizabeth
– on 2 July instead of 31 May

The Blessed Virgin Mary
– on 8 September (or transferred to 9 September) instead of 15 August

If any of the four festivals is celebrated on the alternative date these provisions should be used on the principal date:

Holy Communion	Morning Prayer	Evening Prayer
If Matthias the Apostle is celebrated on Saturday 24 February, the following provision is used on Tuesday 14 May (W):		
Acts 20.17–27	Psalms 98, **99**, 100 or **106*** (or 103)	Psalm **68** or **107***
Psalm 68.9–10, 18–19	Numbers 22.36—23.12	Deuteronomy 31.14–29
John 17.1–11	Luke 8.1–15	1 John 3.1–10
	*1 Samuel 10.1–10; 1 Corinthians 12.1–13	
If The Visit of the Blessed Virgin Mary to Elizabeth is celebrated on Tuesday 2 July, the following provision is used on Friday 31 May (G):		
1 Peter 4.7–13	Psalms 17, **19**	Psalm 22
Psalm 96.10–end	Joshua 9.3–26	Job 11
Mark 11.11–26	Luke 11.29–36	Romans 6.1–14
If Thomas the Apostle is celebrated on Thursday 21 December 2023, the following provision is used on Wednesday 3 July 2024 (G):		
Amos 5.14–15, 21–24	Psalms 110, **111**, 112	Psalm 119.**129–152**
Psalm 50.7–14	1 Samuel 2.12–26	Ezekiel 2.3—3.11
Matthew 8.28–end	Luke 20.1–8	2 Corinthians 2.5–end
If The Blessed Virgin Mary is celebrated on Sunday 8 September, the following provision is used on Thursday 15 August (G):		
Ezekiel 12.1–12	Psalms 90, **92**	Psalm **94**
Psalm 78.58–64	2 Samuel 7.1–17	Proverbs 10.1–12
Matthew 18.21—19.1	Acts 7.44–53	Mark 6.1–13

Key to the Tables

For guidance on how the options for saying the psalms are expressed typographically, see page 5.

Sundays (and Principal Feasts, other Principal Holy Days, and Festivals)

		Principal Service	3rd Service	2nd Service
Day	**Date** Sunday / Feast † / Festival ††	Colour	Main service of the day: Holy Communion, Morning Prayer, Evening Prayer, or a Service of the Word	Shorter Readings, an Office lectionary probably used at Morning Prayer where Holy Communion is the Principal Service	2nd main service, probably used at Evening Prayer; adaptable for Holy Communion

† Principal Feasts and other Principal Holy Days are printed in **bold**.
†† Festivals are printed in roman typeface.

Weekdays

		Holy Communion	Morning Prayer	Evening Prayer
Day	**Date**	Colour	Weekday readings	Psalms and readings for Morning Prayer	Psalms and readings for Evening Prayer

Lesser Festival ‡* [optional]
Commemoration ‡‡ [optional]

‡ Lesser Festivals are printed in roman typeface, in black.
‡‡ Commemorations are printed in *italics*.
* The ascriptions given to holy men and women in the Calendar (such as martyr, teacher of the faith, etc.) have often been abbreviated in this booklet for reasons of space. The particular ascription given is there to be helpful if needing to choose Collects and readings from Common of the Saints; where several ascriptions are used (e.g. bishop and martyr), traditionally the last ascription given is the most important and therefore the guiding one. The full ascriptions may be found in the Calendar, which is printed in *Common Worship: Times and Seasons* (pages 7–22), *Common Worship: Festivals* (pages 5–20) and *Common Worship: Daily Prayer* (pages 5–16). *Common Worship: Daily Prayer* (pages 5–16). These incorporate minor corrections made since the publication of the Calendar in *Common Worship: Services and Prayers for the Church of England* (pages 5–16).

	Principal Service	3rd Service	2nd Service
Sunday 3 December *P* 1st Sunday of Advent	Isaiah 64.1–9 Psalm 80.1–8, 18–20 [or 80.1–8] 1 Corinthians 1.3–9 Mark 13.24–end	*Morning Prayer* Psalm 44 Isaiah 2.1–5 Luke 12.35–48	Psalm 25 [or 25.1–9] Isaiah 1.1–20 Matthew 21.1–13
Monday 4 December *P* John of Damascus, monk, teacher of the faith, c.749 Nicholas Ferrar, deacon, founder of the Little Gidding Community, 1637	*Holy Communion* Isaiah 2.1–5 Psalm 122 Matthew 8.5–11	Psalms 50, 54 or 1, 2, 3 Isaiah 25.1–9 Matthew 12.1–21	*Evening Prayer* Psalms 70, 71 or 4, 7 Isaiah 42.18–end Revelation 19
Tuesday 5 December *P*	Isaiah 11.1–10 Psalm 72.1–4, 18–19 Luke 10.21–24	Psalms **80**, 82 or **5**, 6 (8) Isaiah 26.1–13 Matthew 12.22–37	Psalms **74**, 75 or 9, **10*** Isaiah 43.1–13 Revelation 20
Wednesday 6 December *Pw* Nicholas, bishop, c.326 (see p.81)	Isaiah 25.6–10a Psalm 23 Matthew 15.29–37	Psalms 5, 7 or 119.**1–32** Isaiah 28.1–13 Matthew 12.38–end	Psalms 76, **77** or 11, 12, 13 Isaiah 43.14–end Revelation 21.1–8
Thursday 7 December *Pw* Ambrose, bishop, teacher of the faith, 397 (see p.80)	Isaiah 26.1–6 Psalm 118.18–27a Matthew 7.21, 24–27	Psalms **42**, 43 or 14, **15**, 16 Isaiah 28.14–end Matthew 13.1–23	Psalms **40**, 46 or **18*** Isaiah 44.1–8 Revelation 21.9–21
Friday 8 December *Pw* Conception of the Blessed Virgin Mary (see p.79)	Isaiah 29.17–end Psalm 27.1–4, 16–17 Matthew 9.27–31	Psalms **25**, 26 or 17, **19** Isaiah 29.1–14 Matthew 13.24–43	Psalms 16, **17** or 22 Isaiah 44.9–23 Revelation 21.22—22.5
Saturday 9 December *P*	Isaiah 30.19–21, 23–26 Psalm 146.4–9 Matthew 9.35—10.1, 6–8	Psalms **9**, 10 or 20, 21, **23** Isaiah 29.15–end Matthew 13.44–end	Psalms **27**, 28 or 24, 25 Isaiah 44.24—45.13 Revelation 22.6–end

Advent 2

	Principal Service	3rd Service	2nd Service
Sunday 10 December *P* 2nd Sunday of Advent	Isaiah 40.1–11 Psalm 85.1–2, 8–end [or 85.8–end] 2 Peter 3.8–15a Mark 1.1–8	Psalm 80 Baruch 5.1–9 or Zephaniah 3.14–end Luke 1.5–20	Psalm 40 [or 40.12–end] 1 Kings 22.1–28 Romans 15.4–13 HC Matthew 11.2–11
	Holy Communion	Morning Prayer	Evening Prayer
Monday 11 December *P*	Isaiah 35 Psalm 85.7–end Luke 5.17–26	Psalm **44** or 27, **30** Isaiah 30.1–18 Matthew 14.1–12	Psalms **144**, 146 or 26, **28**, 29 Isaiah 45.14–end 1 Thessalonians 1
Tuesday 12 December *P*	Isaiah 40.1–11 Psalm 96.1, 10–end Matthew 18.12–14	Psalms **56**, 57 or 32, **36** Isaiah 30.19–end Matthew 14.13–end	Psalms 11, 12, 13 or 33 Isaiah 46 1 Thessalonians 2.1–12
Wednesday 13 December *Pr* Lucy, martyr, 304 (see p.79) *Samuel Johnson, moralist, 1784* Ember Day	Isaiah 40.25–end Psalm 103.8–13 Matthew 11.28–end	Psalms **62**, 63 or 34 Isaiah 31 Matthew 15.1–20	Psalms **10**, 14 or 1**19.33–56** Isaiah 47 1 Thessalonians 2.13–end
Thursday 14 December *Pw* John of the Cross, poet, teacher of the faith, 1591 (see p.80)	Isaiah 41.13–20 Psalm 145.1, 8–13 Matthew 11.11–15	Psalms 53, **54**, 60 or **37*** Isaiah 32 Matthew 15.21–28	Psalm **73** or 39, **40** Isaiah 48.1–11 1 Thessalonians 3
Friday 15 December *P* Ember Day	Isaiah 48.17–19 Psalm 1 Matthew 11.16–19	Psalms 85, **86** or 31 Isaiah 33.1–22 Matthew 15.29–end	Psalms 82, **90** or **35** Isaiah 48.12–end 1 Thessalonians 4.1–12
Saturday 16 December *P* Ember Day	Ecclesiasticus 48.1–4, 9–11 or 2 Kings 2.9–12 Psalm 80.1–4, 18–19 Matthew 17.10–13	Psalm **145** or 41, **42**, 43 Isaiah 35 Matthew 16.1–12	Psalms 93, **94** or 45, **46** Isaiah 49.1–13 1 Thessalonians 4.13–end

		Principal Service	3rd Service	2nd Service
Sunday 17 December **3rd Sunday of Advent** *O Sapientia*	P	Isaiah 61.1–4, 8–end Psalm 126 or *Canticle*: Magnificat 1 Thessalonians 5.16–24 John 1.6–8, 19–28	Psalms 50.1–6, 62 Isaiah 12 Luke 1.57–66	Psalm 68.1–19 [or 68.1–8] Malachi 3.1–4; 4 Philippians 4.4–7 HC Matthew 14.1–12
		Holy Communion	*Morning Prayer*	*Evening Prayer*
Monday 18 December	P	Jeremiah 23.5–8 Psalm 72.1–2, 12–13, 18–end Matthew 1.18–24	Psalm **40** or **44** Isaiah 38.1–8, 21–22 Matthew 16.13–end	Psalms 25, **26** or **47**, 49 Isaiah 49.14–25 1 Thessalonians 5.1–11
Tuesday 19 December	P	*From Tuesday 19 December until the Epiphany the seasonal psalmody must be used at Morning and Evening Prayer.* Judges 13.2–7, 24–end Psalm 71.3–8 Luke 1.5–25	Psalms 144, **146** Isaiah 38.9–20 Matthew 17.1–13	Psalms 10, **57** Isaiah 50 1 Thessalonians 5.12–end
Wednesday 20 December	P	Isaiah 7.10–14 Psalm 24.1–6 Luke 1.26–38	Psalms **46**, 95 Isaiah 39 Matthew 17.14–21	Psalms **4**, 9 Isaiah 51.1–8 2 Thessalonians 1
Thursday 21 December	P	Zephaniah 3.14–18 Psalm 33.1–4, 11–12, 20–end Luke 1.39–45	Psalms 121, 122, 123 Zephaniah 1.1—2.3 Matthew 17.22–end	Psalms 80, **84** Isaiah 51.9–16 2 Thessalonians 2
Friday 22 December	P	1 Samuel 1.24–end Psalm 113 Luke 1.46–56	Psalms **124**, 125, 126, 127 Zephaniah 3.1–13 Matthew 18.1–20	Psalms 24, **48** Isaiah 51.17–end 2 Thessalonians 3
Saturday 23 December	P	Malachi 3.1–4, 4.5–end Psalm 25.3–9 Luke 1.57–66	Psalms 128, 129, **130**, 131 Zephaniah 3.14–end Matthew 18.21–end	Psalm **89.1–37** Isaiah 52.1–12 Jude

Advent 4

		Principal Service	3rd Service	2nd Service
Sunday	*P*	2 Samuel 7.1–11,16	Psalm 144	**EP of Christmas Eve**
24 December		*Canticle:* Magnificat	Isaiah 7.10–16	Psalm 85
4th Sunday of Advent		*or* Psalm 89.1–4, 19–26 [*or* 89.1–8]	Romans 1.1–7	Zechariah 2
Christmas Eve		Romans 16.25–end		Revelation 1.1–8
		Luke 1.26–38		
Monday	*Gold or W*	Any of the following three sets of Principal Service readings may be used on the	*MP* Psalms **110**, 117	*EP* Psalm 8
25 December		evening of Christmas Eve and on Christmas Day. Set III should be used at some	Isaiah 62.1–5	Isaiah 65.17–25
Christmas Day		service during the celebration.	Matthew 1.18–end	Philippians 2.5–11
		Set I **Set II** **Set III**		*or* Luke 2.1–20 *if it has not been*
		Isaiah 9.2–7 Isaiah 62.6–end Isaiah 52.7–10		*used at the Principal Service of*
		Psalm 96 Psalm 97 Psalm 98		*the day*
		Titus 2.11–14 Titus 3.4–7 Hebrews 1.1–4 [5–12]		
		Luke 2.1–14 [15–20] Luke 2.[1–7] 8–20 John 1.1–14		
Tuesday	*R*	2 Chronicles 24.20–22 *or* Acts 7.51–end	*MP* Psalms **13**, 31.1–8, 150	*EP* Psalms 57, **86**
26 December		Psalm 119.161–168	Jeremiah 26.12–15	Genesis 4.1–10
Stephen, deacon, first martyr		Acts 7.51–end *or* Galatians 2.16b–20	Acts 6	Matthew 23.34–end
		Matthew 10.17–22		
Wednesday	*W*	Exodus 33.7–11a	*MP* Psalms **21**, 147.13–end	*EP* Psalm **97**
27 December		Psalm 117	Exodus 33.12–end	Isaiah 6.1–8
John, Apostle and Evangelist		1 John 1	1 John 2.1–11	1 John 5.1–12
		John 21.19b–end		
Thursday	*R*	Jeremiah 31.15–17	*MP* Psalms **36**, 146	*EP* Psalms 123, **128**
28 December		Psalm 124	Baruch 4.21–27	Isaiah 49.14–25
The Holy Innocents		1 Corinthians 1.26–29	*or* Genesis 37.13–20	Mark 10.13–16
		Matthew 2.13–18	Matthew 18.1–10	
		Holy Communion	Morning Prayer	Evening Prayer
Friday	*Wr*	1 John 2.3–11	Psalms **19**, 20	Psalms 131, **132**
29 December		Psalm 96.1–4	Jonah 1	Isaiah 57.15–end
Thomas Becket, archbishop, martyr, 1170		Luke 2.22–35	Colossians 1.1–14	John 1.1–18
(see p.79)				
Saturday	*W*	1 John 2.12–17	Psalms 111, 112, **113**	Psalms **65**, 84
30 December		Psalm 96.7–10	Jonah 2	Isaiah 59.1–15a
		Luke 2.36–40	Colossians 1.15–23	John 1.19–28

Christmas 1

		Principal Service	3rd Service	2nd Service
Sunday	**31 December** W **1st Sunday of Christmas**	Isaiah 61.10—62.3 Psalm 148 [or 148.7–end] Galatians 4.4–7 Luke 2.15–21	Psalm 105.1–11 Isaiah 63.7–9 Ephesians 3.5–12	Psalm 132 Isaiah 35 Colossians 1.9–20 or Luke 2.41–end
				or: 1st EP of the Naming and Circumcision of Jesus: Psalm 148; Jeremiah 23.1–6; Colossians 2.8–15
Monday	**1 January** W Naming and Circumcision of Jesus	Numbers 6.22–end Psalm 8 Galatians 4.4–7 Luke 2.15–21	*MP* Psalms **103**, 150 Genesis 17.1–13 Romans 2.17–end	*EP* Psalm **115** Deuteronomy 30. [1–10] 11–end Acts 3.1–16
		Holy Communion	**Morning Prayer**	**Evening Prayer**
Tuesday	**2 January** W Basil the Great and Gregory of Nazianzus, bishops, teachers of the faith, 379 and 389 (see p.80) *Seraphim, monk, spiritual guide, 1833 Vedanayagam Samuel Azariah, bishop, evangelist, 1945*	1 John 2.22–28 Psalm 98.1–4 John 1.19–28	Psalm 18.1–30 Ruth 1 Colossians 2.8–end	Psalms 45, **46** Isaiah 60.1–12 John 1.35–42

Epiphany / Baptism of Christ

If the Epiphany is celebrated on Saturday 6 January and the Baptism of Christ is celebrated on Sunday 7 January:

		Holy Communion	Morning Prayer	Evening Prayer
Wednesday 3 January	W	1 John 2.29—3.6 Psalm 98.2–7 John 1.29–34	Psalms **127**, 128, 131 Ruth 2 Colossians 3.1–11	Psalms **2**, 110 Isaiah 60.13–end John 1.43–end
Thursday 4 January	W	1 John 3.7–10 Psalm 98.1, 8–end John 1.35–42	Psalm **89**.1–37 Ruth 3 Colossians 3.12—4.1	Psalms 85, **87** Isaiah 61 John 2.1–12
Friday 5 January	W	1 John 3.11–21 Psalm 100 John 1.43–end	Psalms 8, **48** Ruth 4.1–17 Colossians 4.2–end	**1st EP of the Epiphany** Psalms 96, **97** Isaiah 49.1–13 John 4.7–26
		Principal Service	*3rd Service*	*2nd Service*
Saturday 6 January Epiphany	Gold or W	Isaiah 60.1–6 Psalm 72.[1–9] 10–15 Ephesians 3.1–12 Matthew 2.1–12	MP Psalms **132**, 113 Jeremiah 31.7–14 John 1.29–34	EP Psalms **98**, 100 Baruch 4.36—end of 5 or Isaiah 60.1–9 John 2.1–11
		Holy Communion	*3rd Service*	*2nd Service*
Sunday 7 January Baptism of Christ 1st Sunday of Epiphany	Gold or W	Genesis 1.1–5 Psalm 29 Acts 19.1–7 Mark 1.4–11	Psalm 89.19–29 1 Samuel 16.1–3, 13 John 1.29–34	Psalms 46 [**47**] Isaiah 42.1–9 Ephesians 2.1–10 HC Matthew 3.13–end
		Holy Communion	*Morning Prayer*	*Evening Prayer*
Monday 8 January DEL week 1	W	1 Samuel 1.1–8 Psalm 116.10–15 Mark 1.14–20	Psalms **2**, 110 or 71 Genesis 1.1–19 Matthew 21.1–17	Psalms 34, 36 or **72**, 75 Amos 1 1 Corinthians 1.1–17

Epiphany / Baptism of Christ

If the Epiphany is celebrated on Sunday 7 January and the Baptism of Christ is transferred to Monday 8 January:

		Holy Communion	Principal Service	Morning Prayer	Evening Prayer
Wednesday 3 January	W	1 John 2.29—3.6 Psalm 98.2–7 John 1.29–34		Psalms **127**, 128, 131 Ruth 2 Colossians 3.1–11	Psalms **2**, 110 Isaiah 60.13–end John 1.43–end
Thursday 4 January	W	1 John 3.7–10 Psalm 98.1, 8–end John 1.35–42		Psalm **89.1–37** Ruth 3 Colossians 3.12—4.1	Psalms 85, **87** Isaiah 61 John 2.1–12
Friday 5 January	W	1 John 3.11–21 Psalm 100 John 1.43–end		Psalms 8, **48** Ruth 4.1–17 Colossians 4.2–end	Psalms 96, **97** Isaiah 62 John 2.13–end
Saturday 6 January	W	1 John 5.5–13 Psalm 147.13–end Mark 1.7–11		Psalms **99**, 147.1–12 Baruch 1.15–2.10 or Jeremiah 23.1–8 Matthew 20.1–16	**1st EP of the Epiphany** Psalms 96, **97** Isaiah 49.1–13 John 4.7–26

		Principal Service	3rd Service		2nd Service
Sunday 7 January Epiphany	*Gold or W*	Isaiah 60.1–6 Psalm 72. [1–9] 10–15 Ephesians 3.1–12 Matthew 2.1–12	MP Psalms **132**, 113 Jeremiah 31.7–14 John 1.29–34		EP Psalms **98**, 100 Baruch 4.36—end of 5 or Isaiah 60.1–9 John 2.1–11
Monday 8 January Baptism of Christ	*Gold or W*	Genesis 1.1–5 Psalm 29 Acts 19.1–7 Mark 1.4–11	Psalm 89.19–29 1 Samuel 16.1–3, 13 John 1.29–34		Psalms 46 [47] Isaiah 42.1–9 Ephesians 2.1–10 HC Matthew 3.13–end

Epiphany I

		Holy Communion	Morning Prayer	Evening Prayer
Tuesday	**9 January** W	1 Samuel 1.9–20	Psalms 8, **9** or **73**	Psalms **45**, 46 or **74**
	DEL week 1	*Canticle:* 1 Samuel 2.1, 4–8 or Magnificat	Genesis 1.20—2.3	Amos 2
		Mark 1.21–28	Matthew 21.18–32	1 Corinthians 1.1–18
Wednesday	**10 January** W	1 Samuel 3.1–10, 19–20	Psalms 19, **20** or **77**	Psalms **47**, 48 or **119.81–104**
	William Laud, archbishop, 1645	Psalm 40.1–4, 7–10	Genesis 2.4–end	Amos 3
		Mark 1.29–39	Matthew 21.33–end	1 Corinthians 2
Thursday	**11 January** W	1 Samuel 4.1–11	Psalms 21, 24 or **78.1–39***	Psalms **61**, 65 or **78.40–end***
	Mary Slessor, missionary, 1915	Psalm 44.10–15, 24–25	Genesis 3	Amos 4
		Mark 1.40–end	Matthew 22.1–14	1 Corinthians 3
Friday	**12 January** W	1 Samuel 8.4–7, 10–end	Psalms **67**, 72 or **55**	Psalm **68** or **69**
	Aelred, abbot, 1167 (see p.82)	Psalm 89.15–18	Genesis 4.1–16, 25–26	Amos 5.1–17
	Benedict Biscop, scholar, 689	Mark 2.1–12	Matthew 22.15–33	1 Corinthians 4
Saturday	**13 January** W	1 Samuel 9.1–4, 17–19, 10.1*a*	Psalms 29, **33** or **76**, 79	Psalms 84, **85** or 81, **84**
	Hilary, bishop, teacher of the faith, 367 (see p.80)	Psalm 21.1–6	Genesis 6.1–10	Amos 5.18–end
	Kentigern (Mungo), missionary bishop, 603	Mark 2.13–17	Matthew 22.34–end	1 Corinthians 5
	George Fox, founder of the Society of Friends (Quakers), 1691			

Epiphany 2

	Principal Service	3rd Service	2nd Service
Sunday 14 January W **2nd Sunday of Epiphany**	*Holy Communion* 1 Samuel 3.1–10 [11–20] Psalm 139.1–5, 12–18 [or 139.1–9] Revelation 5.1–10 John 1.43–end	*Morning Prayer* Psalm 145.1–12 Isaiah 62.1–5 1 Corinthians 6.11–end	Psalm 96 Isaiah 60.9–end Hebrews 6.17—7.10 HC Matthew 8.5–13 *Evening Prayer*
Monday 15 January W DEL week 2	1 Samuel 15.16–23 Psalm 50.8–10, 16–17, 24 Mark 2.18–22	Psalms 145, **146** or **80**, 82 Genesis 6.11—7.10 Matthew 24.1–14	Psalm **71** or **85**, 86 Amos 6 1 Corinthians 6.1–11
Tuesday 16 January W	1 Samuel 16.1–13 Psalm 89.19–27 Mark 2.23–end	Psalms **132**, 147.1–12 or 87, **89**.1–18 Genesis 7.11–end Matthew 24.15–28	Psalm **89**.1–37 or **89**.19–end Amos 7 1 Corinthians 6.12–end
Wednesday 17 January W Antony of Egypt, hermit, abbot, 356 (see p.82) *Charles Gore, bishop, founder of the* *Community of the Resurrection, 1932*	1 Samuel 17.32–33, 37, 40–51 Psalm 144.1–2, 9–10 Mark 3.1–6	Psalms **81**, 147.13–end or **119**.105–128 Genesis 8.1–14 Matthew 24.29–end	Psalms **97**, 98 or **91**, 93 Amos 8 1 Corinthians 7.1–24
Thursday 18 January W **Week of Prayer for Christian Unity:** **18–25 January** *Amy Carmichael, spiritual writer, 1951*	1 Samuel 18.6–9, 19.1–7 Psalm 56.1–2, 8–end Mark 3.7–12	Psalms **76**, 148 or 90, **92** Genesis 8.15—9.7 Matthew 25.1–13	Psalms 99, 100, 111 or **94** Amos 9 1 Corinthians 7.25–end
Friday 19 January W Wulfstan, bishop, 1095 (see p.81)	1 Samuel 24.3–22a Psalm 57.1–2, 8–end Mark 3.13–19	Psalms **27**, 149 or **88** (95) Genesis 9.8–19 Matthew 25.14–30	Psalm **73** or **102** Hosea 1.1—2.1 1 Corinthians 8
Saturday 20 January W *Richard Rolle, spiritual writer, 1349*	2 Samuel 1.1–4, 11–12, 17–19, 23–end Psalm 80.1–6 Mark 3.20–21	Psalms **122**, 128, 150 or 96, **97**, 100 Genesis 11.1–9 Matthew 25.31–end	Psalms **61**, 66 or **104** Hosea 2.2–17 1 Corinthians 9.1–14

		Principal Service	3rd Service	2nd Service
Sunday	**21 January** **3rd Sunday of Epiphany**	W	Genesis 14.17–20 Psalm 128 Revelation 19.6–10 John 2.1–11	Psalm 113 Jonah 3.1–5,10 John 3.16–21	Psalm 33 [or 33.1–12] Jeremiah 3.21—4.2 Titus 2.1–8, 11–14 HC Matthew 4.12–23
			Holy Communion	Morning Prayer	Evening Prayer
Monday	**22 January** *Vincent of Saragossa, deacon, martyr, 304* DEL week 3	W	2 Samuel 5.1–7, 10 Psalm 89.19–27 Mark 3.22–30	Psalms 40, 108 or 98, 99, 101 Genesis 11.27—12.9 Matthew 26.1–16	Psalms 138, 144 or 105* (or 103) Hosea 2.18—end of 3 1 Corinthians 9.15–end
Tuesday	**23 January**	W	2 Samuel 6.12–15, 17–19 Psalm 24.7–end Mark 3.31–end	Psalms 34, 36 or 106* (or 103) Genesis 13.2–end Matthew 26.17–35	Psalm 145 or 107* Hosea 4.1–16 1 Corinthians 10.1–13
Wednesday	**24 January** Francis de Sales, bishop, teacher of the faith, 1622 (see p.80)	W	2 Samuel 7.4–17 Psalm 89.19–27 Mark 4.1–20	Psalms 45, 46 or 110, 111, 112 Genesis 14 Matthew 26.36–46	Psalm 21, **29** or 119.**129–152** Hosea 5.1–7 1 Corinthians 10.14—11.1 *or*: 1st EP of the Conversion of Paul: Psalm 149; Isaiah 49.1–1; Acts 22.3–16
			Principal Service	3rd Service	2nd Service
Thursday	**25 January** Conversion of Paul	W	Jeremiah 1.4–10 or Acts 9.1–22 Psalm 67 Acts 9.1–22 or Galatians 1.11–16a Matthew 19.27–end	MP Psalms 66, 147.13–end Ezekiel 3.22–end Philippians 3.1–14	EP Psalm 119.41–56 Ecclesiasticus 39.1–10 or Isaiah 56.1–8 Colossians 1.24—2.7
			Holy Communion	Morning Prayer	Evening Prayer
Friday	**26 January** Timothy and Titus, companions of Paul	W	2 Samuel 11.1–10, 13–17 Psalm 51.1–6, 9 Mark 4.26–34 *Lesser Festival eucharistic lectionary:* Isaiah 61.1–3a Psalm 100 1 Timothy 2.1–8 or Titus 1.1–5 Luke 10.1–9	Psalms 61, 65 or 139 Genesis 16 Matthew 26.57–end	Psalms 67, 77 or 130, 131, 137 Hosea 6.7—7.2 1 Corinthians 11.17–end

19

Epiphany 4 / Presentation

If the Presentation of Christ is celebrated on Friday 2 February:

Saturday 27 January — W

	Holy Communion	Morning Prayer / 3rd Service	Evening Prayer / 2nd Service
	2 Samuel 12.1–7, 10–17 Psalm 51.1–16 Mark 4.35–end	Psalm 68 or 120, 121, 122 Genesis 17.1–16 Matthew 27.1–10	Psalms 72, 76 or 118 Hosea 8 1 Corinthians 12.1–11

Sunday 28 January — W — 4th Sunday of Epiphany

	Principal Service	Morning Prayer / 3rd Service	Evening Prayer / 2nd Service
	Deuteronomy 18.15–20 Psalm 111 Revelation 12.1–5a Mark 1.21–28	Psalm 71.1–6, 15–17 Jeremiah 1.4–10 Mark 1.40–end	Psalm 34 [or 34.1–10] 1 Samuel 3.1–20 1 Corinthians 14.12–20 HC Matthew 13.10–17

Monday 29 January — W — DEL week 4

	Holy Communion	Morning Prayer	Evening Prayer
	2 Samuel 15.13–14, 30; 16.5–13 Psalm 3 Mark 5.1–20	Psalms 57, 96 or 123, 124, 125, **126** Genesis 18.1–15 Matthew 27.11–26	Psalms 2, **20** or **127**, **128**, 129 Hosea 9 1 Corinthians 12.12–end

Tuesday 30 January — Wr — Charles, king and martyr, 1649 (see p.79)

	Holy Communion	Morning Prayer	Evening Prayer
	2 Samuel 18.9–10, 14, 24–25, 30—19.3 Psalm 86.1–6 Mark 5.21–end	Psalms 93, 97 or **132**, 133 Genesis 18.16–end Matthew 27.27–44	Psalms **19**, 21 or (**134**,) **135** Hosea 10 1 Corinthians 13

Wednesday 31 January — W — John Bosco, priest, founder of the Salesian Teaching Order, 1888

	Holy Communion	Morning Prayer	Evening Prayer
	2 Samuel 24.2, 9–17 Psalm 32.1–8 Mark 6.1–6a	Psalms **95**, 98 or 119.**153–end** Genesis 19.1–3, 12–29 Matthew 27.45–56	Psalms **81**, 111 or **136** Hosea 11.1–11 1 Corinthians 14.1–19

Thursday 1 February — W — Brigid, abbess, c.525

	Holy Communion	Morning Prayer	Evening Prayer
	1 Kings 2.1–4, 10–12 Canticle: 1 Chronicles 29.10–12 or Psalm 145.1–5 Mark 6.7–13	Psalms 99, **110** or 143, 146 Genesis 21.1–21 Matthew 27.57–end	**1st EP of the Presentation** Psalm 118 1 Samuel 1.19b–end Hebrews 4.11–end

Friday 2 February — Gold or W — Presentation of Christ in the Temple (Candlemas)

	Principal Service	Morning Prayer / 3rd Service	Evening Prayer / 2nd Service
	Malachi 3.1–5 Psalm 24. [1–6] 7–end Hebrews 2.14–end Luke 2.22–40	MP Psalms **48**, 146 Exodus 13.1–16 Romans 12.1–5	EP Psalms 122, **132** Haggai 2.1–9 John 2.18–22

Saturday 3 February — Gw — Anskar, archbishop, missionary, 865 (see p.82)
Ordinary Time begins today
The Collect of 5 before Lent is used
DEL week 4

	Holy Communion	Morning Prayer	Evening Prayer
	1 Kings 3.4–13 Psalm 119.9–16 Mark 6.30–34	Psalm **147** Genesis 23 Matthew 28.16–end	Psalms **148**, 149, 150 Hosea 14 1 Corinthians 16.10–end

Presentation / Epiphany 4

If the Presentation of Christ is transferred to Sunday 28 January:

		Holy Communion	Morning Prayer	Evening Prayer
Saturday 27 January	W	2 Samuel 12.1–7, 10–17 Psalm 51.11–16 Mark 4.35–end	Psalm **68** or 120, **121**, 122 Genesis 17.1–22 Matthew 27.1–10	**1st EP of the Presentation** Psalm 118 1 Samuel 1.19b–end Hebrews 4.11–end
		Principal Service	**3rd Service**	**2nd Service**
Sunday 28 January Presentation of Christ in the Temple (Candlemas)	*Gold or W*	Malachi 3.1–5 Psalm 24.[1–6] 7–end Hebrews 2.14–end Luke 2.22–40	MP Psalms **48**, 146 Exodus 13.1–16 Romans 12.1–5	EP Psalms 122, **132** Haggai 2.1–9 John 2.18–22
		Holy Communion	**Morning Prayer**	**Evening Prayer**
Monday 29 January Ordinary Time begins today The Collect of 5 before Lent is used DEL week 4	G	2 Samuel 15.13–14, 30, 16.5–13 Psalm 3 Mark 5.1–20	Psalms 123, 124, 125, **126** Genesis 18.1–15 Matthew 27.11–26	Psalms **127**, 128, 129 Hosea 9 1 Corinthians 12.12–end
Tuesday 30 January Charles, king and martyr, 1649 (see p.79)	Gr	2 Samuel 18.9–10, 14, 24–25, 30—19.3 Psalm 86.1–6 Mark 5.21–end	Psalms **132**, 133 Genesis 18.16–end Matthew 27.27–44	Psalms (134,) **135** Hosea 10 1 Corinthians 13
Wednesday 31 January John Bosco, priest, founder of the Salesian Teaching Order, 1888	G	2 Samuel 24.2, 9–17 Psalm 32.1–8 Mark 6.1–6a	Psalm 119.**153–end** Genesis 19.1–3, 12–29 Matthew 27.45–56	Psalm **136** Hosea 11.1–11 1 Corinthians 14.1–19
Thursday 1 February Brigid, abbess, c.525	G	1 Kings 2.1–4, 10–12 *Canticle:* 1 Chronicles 29.10–12 or Psalm 145.1–5 Mark 6.7–13	Psalms **143**, 146 Genesis 21.1–21 Matthew 27.57–end	Psalms **138**, 140, 141 Hosea 11.12—end of 12 1 Corinthians 14.20–end
Friday 2 February	G	Ecclesiasticus 47.2–11 Psalm 18.31–36, 50–end Mark 6.14–29	Psalms 142, **144** Genesis 22.1–19 Matthew 28.1–15	Psalm **145** Hosea 13.1–14 1 Corinthians 16.1–9
Saturday 3 February Anskar, archbishop, missionary, 865 (see p.82)	Gw	1 Kings 3.4–13 Psalm 119.9–16 Mark 6.30–34	Psalm **147** Genesis 23 Matthew 28.16–end	Psalms **148**, 149, 150 Hosea 14 1 Corinthians 16.10–end

2 before Lent

		Principal Service	3rd Service	2nd Service
Sunday	**4 February** G **2nd Sunday before Lent**	Proverbs 8.1, 22–31 Psalm 104.26–end Colossians 1.15–20 John 1.1–14	Psalms 29, 67 Deuteronomy 8.1–10 Matthew 6.25–end	Psalm 65 Genesis 2.4b–end Luke 8.22–35
		Holy Communion	*Morning Prayer*	*Evening Prayer*
Monday	**5 February** G DEL week 5	1 Kings 8.1–7, 9–13 Psalm 132.1–9 Mark 6.53–end	Psalms 1, **2**, **3** Genesis 29.31—30.24 2 Timothy 4.1–8	Psalms **4**, 7 Ecclesiastes 7.1–14 John 19.1–16
Tuesday	**6 February** G *Martyrs of Japan, 1597*	1 Kings 8.22–23, 27–30 Psalm 84.1–10 Mark 7.1–13	Psalms **5**, 6 (8) Genesis 31.1–24 2 Timothy 4.9–end	Psalms **9**, 10 Ecclesiastes 7.15–end John 19.17–30
Wednesday	**7 February** G	1 Kings 10.1–10 Psalm 37.3–6, 30–32 Mark 7.14–23	Psalm 1**19.1–32** Genesis 31.25—32.2 Titus 1	Psalms 1**1**, 12, 13 Ecclesiastes 8 John 19.31–end
Thursday	**8 February** G	1 Kings 11.4–13 Psalm 106.3, 35–41 Mark 7.24–30	Psalms 14, **15**, 16 Genesis 32.3–30 Titus 2	Psalm **18*** Ecclesiastes 9 John 20.1–10
Friday	**9 February** G	1 Kings 11.29–32; 12.19 Psalm 81.8–14 Mark 7.31–end	Psalms 17, **19** Genesis 33.1–17 Titus 3	Psalm **22** Ecclesiastes 11.1–8 John 20.11–18
Saturday	**10 February** G *Scholastica, abbess, c.543*	1 Kings 12.26–32; 13.33–end Psalm 106.6–7, 20–23 Mark 8.1–10	Psalms 20, 21, **23** Genesis 35 Philemon	Psalms **24**, 25 Ecclesiastes 11.9—end of 12 John 20.19–end

Sunday next before Lent

		Principal Service	3rd Service	2nd Service
Sunday 11 February Sunday next before Lent	G	2 Kings 2.1–12 Psalm 50.1–6 2 Corinthians 4.3–6 Mark 9.2–9	Psalms 27, 150 Exodus 24.12–end 2 Corinthians 3.12–end	Psalms 2 [99] 1 Kings 19.1–16 2 Peter 1.16–end HC Mark 9.[2–8] 9–13
		Holy Communion	**Morning Prayer**	**Evening Prayer**
Monday 12 February DEL week 6	G	James 1.1–11 Psalm 119.65–72 Mark 8.11–13	Psalms 27, **30** Genesis 37.1–11 Galatians 1	Psalms 26, **28**, 29 Jeremiah 1 John 3.1–21
Tuesday 13 February	G	James 1.12–18 Psalm 94.12–18 Mark 8.14–21	Psalms 32, **36** Genesis 37.12–end Galatians 2.1–10	Psalm 33 Jeremiah 2.1–13 John 3.22–end
		Principal Service	**3rd Service**	**2nd Service**
Wednesday 14 February Ash Wednesday	P(La)	Joel 2.1–2, 12–17 or Isaiah 58.1–12 Psalm 51.1–18 2 Corinthians 5.20b—6.10 Matthew 6.1–6, 16–21 or John 8.1–11	MP Psalm 38 Daniel 9.3–6, 17–19 1 Timothy 6.6–19	EP Psalm **51** or 102 [or 102.1–18] Isaiah 1.10–18 Luke 15.11–end
		Holy Communion	**Morning Prayer**	**Evening Prayer**
Thursday 15 February *Sigfrid, bishop, 1045* *Thomas Bray, priest,* *founder of SPCK and SPG, 1730*	P(La)	Deuteronomy 30.15–end Psalm 1 Luke 9.22–25	Psalm 77 or 37* Genesis 39 Galatians 2.11–end	Psalm 74 or 39, **40** Jeremiah 2.14–32 John 4.1–26
Friday 16 February	P(La)	Isaiah 58.1–9a Psalm 51.1–5, 17–18 Matthew 9.14–15	Psalms **3**, 7 or 31 Genesis 40 Galatians 3.1–14	Psalm 31 or **35** Jeremiah 3.6–22 John 4.27–42
Saturday 17 February *Janani Luwum, archbishop, martyr, 1977* (see p.79)	P(La)r	Isaiah 58.9b–end Psalm 86.1–7 Luke 5.27–32	Psalm 71 or 41, **42**, 43 Genesis 41.1–24 Galatians 3.15–22	Psalm 73 or 45, **46** Jeremiah 4.1–18 John 4.43–end

		Principal Service	3rd Service	2nd Service
Sunday	*P(La)*	Genesis 9.8–17	Psalm 77	Psalm 119.17–32
18 February		Psalm 25.1–9	Exodus 34.1–10	Genesis 2.15–17; 3.1–7
1st Sunday of Lent		1 Peter 3.18–end	Romans 10.8b–13	Romans 5.12–19
		Mark 1.9–15		or Luke 13.31–end
		Holy Communion	**Morning Prayer**	**Evening Prayer**
Monday	*P(La)*	Leviticus 19.1–2, 11–18	Psalms 10, 11 or **44**	Psalms 12, **13**, 14 or **47**, 49
19 February		Psalm 19.7–end	Genesis 41.25–45	Jeremiah 4.19–end
		Matthew 25.31–end	Galatians 3.23—4.7	Galatians 5.1–18
Tuesday	*P(La)*	Isaiah 55.10–11	Psalm **44** or **48**, 52	Psalms 46, **49** or **50**
20 February		Psalm 34.4–6, 21–22	Genesis 41.46—42.5	Jeremiah 5.1–19
		Matthew 6.7–15	Galatians 4.8–20	John 5.19–29
Wednesday	*P(La)*	Jonah 3	Psalms **6**, 17 or 1**19.57–80**	Psalms 9, **28** or **59**, 60 (67)
21 February		Psalm 51.1–5, 17–18	Genesis 42.6–17	Jeremiah 5.20–end
Ember Day		Luke 11.29–32	Galatians 4.21—5.1	John 5.30–end
Thursday	*P(La)*	Esther 14.1–5, 12–14	Psalms **42**, 43 or 56, **57** (63*)	Psalms 137, **138**, **142** or 61, **62**, 64
22 February		or Isaiah 55.6–9	Genesis 42.18–28	Jeremiah 6.9–21
		Psalm 138	Galatians 5.2–15	John 6.1–15
		Matthew 7.7–12		
Friday	*P(La)r*	Ezekiel 18.21–28	Psalm **22** or **51**, 54	Psalms 54, **55** or 38
23 February		Psalm 130	Genesis 42.29–end	Jeremiah 6.22–end
Polycarp, bishop, martyr, c.155 (see p.79)		Matthew 5.20–26	Galatians 5.16–end	John 6.16–27
Ember Day				
Saturday	*P(La)*	Deuteronomy 26.16–end	Psalms 59, **63** or **68**	Psalms **4**, 16 or 65, **66**
24 February		Psalm 119.1–8	Genesis 43.1–15	Jeremiah 7.1–20
Ember Day		Matthew 5.43–end	Galatians 6	John 6.27–40

Lent 2

			Principal Service	3rd Service	2nd Service
Sunday	**25 February** **2nd Sunday of Lent**	P(La)	Genesis 17.1–7, 15–16 Psalm 22.23–end Romans 4.13–end Mark 8.31–end	Psalm 105.1–6, 37–end Isaiah 51.1–11 Galatians 3.1–9, 23–end	Psalm 135 [or 135.1–14] Genesis 12.1–9 Hebrews 11.1–3, 8–16 HC John 8.51–end
			Holy Communion	*Morning Prayer*	*Evening Prayer*
Monday	**26 February**	P(La)	Daniel 9.4–10 Psalm 79.8–9, 12, 14 Luke 6.36–38	Psalms 26, **32** or **71** Genesis 43.16–end Hebrews 1	Psalms 70, **74** or **72**, 75 Jeremiah 7.21–end John 6.41–51
Tuesday	**27 February** George Herbert, priest, poet, 1633 (see p.81)	P(La)w	Isaiah 1.10, 16–20 Psalm 50.8, 16–end Matthew 23.1–12	Psalm **50** or **73** Genesis 44.1–17 Hebrews 2.1–9	Psalms **52**, 53, 54 or **74** Jeremiah 8.1–15 John 6.52–59
Wednesday	**28 February**	P(La)	Jeremiah 18.18–20 Psalm 31.4–5, 14–18 Matthew 20.17–28	Psalm **35** or **77** Genesis 44.18–end Hebrews 2.10–end	Psalms 3, 51 or **119.81–104** Jeremiah 8.18—9.11 John 6.60–end
Thursday	**29 February**	P(La)	Jeremiah 17.5–10 Psalm 1 Luke 16.19–end	Psalm **34** or **78.1–39*** Genesis 45.1–15 Hebrews 3.1–6	Psalm **71** or **78.40–end*** Jeremiah 9.12–24 John 7.1–13
Friday	**1 March** David, bishop, patron of Wales, c.601 (see p.81)	P(La)w	Genesis 37.3–4, 12–13, 17–28 Psalm 105.16–22 Matthew 21.33–43, 45–46	Psalms 40, **41** or **55** Genesis 45.16–end Hebrews 3.7–end	Psalms **6**, 38 or **69** Jeremiah 10.1–16 John 7.14–24
Saturday	**2 March** Chad, bishop, missionary, 672 (see p.82)	P(La)w	Micah 7.14–15, 18–20 Psalm 103.1–4, 9–12 Luke 15.1–3, 11–end	Psalms 3, **25** or 76, 79 Genesis 46.1–7, 28–end Hebrews 4.1–13	Psalms **23**, 27 or 81, **84** Jeremiah 10.17–24 John 7.25–36

Lent 3

		Principal Service	3rd Service	2nd Service
Sunday	**3 March** *P(La)* **3rd Sunday of Lent**	Exodus 20.1–17; Psalm 19 [or 19.7–end]; 1 Corinthians 1.18–25; John 2.13–22	Psalm 18.1–25; Jeremiah 38; Philippians 1.1–26	Psalms 11, 12; Exodus 5.1—6.1; Philippians 3.4b–14 or Matthew 10.16–22
		Holy Communion	Morning Prayer	Evening Prayer

The following readings may replace those provided for Holy Communion on any day during the Third Week of Lent: Exodus 17.1–7; Psalm 95.1–2, 6–end; John 4.5–42

		Holy Communion	Morning Prayer	Evening Prayer
Monday	**4 March** *P(La)*	2 Kings 5.1–15; Psalms 42.1–2; 43.1–4; Luke 4.24–30	Psalms 5, 7 or 80, 82; Genesis 47.1–27; Hebrews 4.14—5.10	Psalms 11, **17** or **85**, 86; Jeremiah 11.1–17; John 7.37–52
Tuesday	**5 March** *P(La)*	Song of the Three 2, 11–20 or Daniel 2.20–23; Psalm 25.3–10; Matthew 18.21–end	Psalms 6, **9** or 87, **89.1–18**; Genesis 47.28—end of 48; Hebrews 5.11—6.12	Psalms 61, 62, **64** or **89.19–end**; Jeremiah 11.18—12.6; John 7.53—8.11
Wednesday	**6 March** *P(La)*	Deuteronomy 4.1, 5–9; Psalm 147.13–end; Matthew 5.17–19	Psalm **38** or **119.105–128**; Genesis 49.1–32; Hebrews 6.13–end	Psalms 36, **39** or **91**, 93; Jeremiah 13.1–11; John 8.12–30
Thursday	**7 March** *P(Lo)r* Perpetua, Felicity and companions, martyrs, 203 (see p.79)	Jeremiah 7.23–28; Psalm 95.1–2, 6–end; Luke 11.14–23	Psalms **56**, 57 or 90, **92**; Genesis 49.33—end of 50; Hebrews 7.1–10	Psalms **59**, 60 or **94**; Jeremiah 14; John 8.31–47
Friday	**8 March** *P(Lo)w* Edward King, bishop, 1910 (see p.81); Felix, bishop, 647; Geoffrey Studdert Kennedy, priest, poet, 1929	Hosea 14; Psalm 81.6–10, 13, 16; Mark 12.28–34	Psalm **22** or **88** (95); Exodus 1.1–14; Hebrews 7.11–end	Psalm **69** or **102**; Jeremiah 15.10–end; John 8.48–end
Saturday	**9 March** *P(La)*	Hosea 5.15—6.6; Psalm 51.1–2, 17–end; Luke 18.9–14	Psalm **31** or 96, **97**, 100; Exodus 1.22—2.10; Hebrews 8	Psalms **116**, 130 or **104**; Jeremiah 16.10—17.4; John 9.1–17

Lent 4

		Principal Service	3rd Service	2nd Service
Sunday	**10 March** P(La) **4th Sunday of Lent**	Numbers 21.4-9 Psalm 107.1-3, 17-22 [or 107.1-9] Ephesians 2.1-10 John 3.14-21	Psalm 27 1 Samuel 16.1-13 John 9.1-25	Psalms 13, 14 Exodus 6.2-13 Romans 5.1-11 HC John 12.1-8

For Mothering Sunday:
Exodus 2.1-10 or 1 Samuel 1.20-end; Psalm 34.11-20 or 127.1-4;
2 Corinthians 1.3-7 or Colossians 3.12-17; Luke 2.33-35 or John 19.25b-27
If the Principal Service readings have been displaced by Mothering Sunday provisions, they may be used at the Second Service.

		Holy Communion	Morning Prayer	Evening Prayer
		The following readings may replace those provided for Holy Communion on any day during the Fourth Week of Lent: Micah 7.7-9; Psalm 27.1, 9-10, 16-17; John 9		
Monday	**11 March** P(La)	Isaiah 65.17-21 Psalm 30.1-5, 8, 11-end John 4.43-end	Psalms 70, 77 or **98**, 99, 101 Exodus 2.11-22 Hebrews 9.1-14	Psalms **25**, 28 or **105*** (or 103) Jeremiah 17.5-18 John 9.18-end
Tuesday	**12 March** P(La)	Ezekiel 47.1-9, 12 Psalm 46.1-8 John 5.1-3, 5-16	Psalms 54, **79** or **106*** (or 103) Exodus 2.23—3.20 Hebrews 9.15-end	Psalms **80**, 82 or **107*** Jeremiah 18.1-12 John 10.1-10
Wednesday	**13 March** P(La)	Isaiah 49.8-15 Psalm 145.8-18 John 5.17-30	Psalms 63, **90** or 110, **111**, 112 Exodus 4.1-23 Hebrews 10.1-18	Psalms 52, **91** or 119.**129—152** Jeremiah 18.13-end John 10.11-21
Thursday	**14 March** P(La)	Exodus 32.7-14 Psalm 106.19-23 John 5.31-end	Psalms 53, **86** or 113, **115** Exodus 4.27—6.1 Hebrews 10.19-25	Psalms **94** or 114, **116**, 117 Jeremiah 19.1-13 John 10.22-end
Friday	**15 March** P(La)	Wisdom 2.1, 12-22 or Jeremiah 26.8-11 Psalm 34.15-end John 7.1-2, 10, 25-30	Psalm **102** or **139** Exodus 6.2-13 Hebrews 10.26-end	Psalms 13, **16** or **130**, **131**, 137 Jeremiah 19.14—20.6 John 11.1-16
Saturday	**16 March** P(La)	Jeremiah 11.18-20 Psalm 7.1-2, 8-10 John 7.40-52	Psalm **32** or 120, **121**, 122 Exodus 7.8-end Hebrews 11.1-16	Psalms **140**, 141, 142 or **118** Jeremiah 20.7-end John 11.17-27

Lent 5

			Principal Service	3rd Service	2nd Service
Sunday	**17 March** **5th Sunday of Lent** *Passiontide begins*	*P(La)*	**Holy Communion** Jeremiah 31.31–34 Psalm 51.1–13 or Psalm 119.9–16 Hebrews 5.5–10 John 12.20–33	**Morning Prayer** Psalm 107.1–22 Exodus 24.3–8 Hebrews 12.18–end	**Evening Prayer** Psalm 34 [or 34.1–10] Exodus 7.8–24 Romans 5.12–end HC Luke 22.1–13
	The following readings may replace those provided for Holy Communion on any day during the Fifth Week of Lent (except the Festival of Joseph of Nazareth): *2 Kings 4.1–8–21, 32–37; Psalm 17.1–8, 16; John 11.1–45*				
Monday	**18 March** *Cyril, bishop, teacher of the faith, 386*	*P(La)*	Susannah 1–9, 15–17, 19–30, 33–62 [or 41b–62] or Joshua 2.1–14 Psalm 23 John 8.1–11	Psalms 73, 121 or 123, 124, 125, **126** Exodus 8.1–19 Hebrews 11.17–31	Psalms **26**, 27 or **127**, 128, 129 Jeremiah 21.1–10 John 11.28–44 or: 1st EP of Joseph of Nazareth: Psalm 132: Hosea 11.1–9; Luke 2.41–end
Tuesday	**19 March** Joseph of Nazareth	W	**Principal Service** 2 Samuel 7.4–16 Psalm 89.26–36 Romans 4.13–18 Matthew 1.18–end	**3rd Service** MP Psalms 25, 147.1–12 Isaiah 11.1–10 Matthew 13.54–end	**2nd Service** EP Psalms 1, 112 Genesis 50.22–end Matthew 2.13–end
Wednesday	**20 March** Cuthbert, bishop, missionary, 687 (see p.82)	*P(La)w*	**Holy Communion** Daniel 3.14–20, 24–25, 28 *Canticle:* Bless the Lord John 8.31–42	**Morning Prayer** Psalms 55, 124 or 119.**153**–end Exodus 9.1–12 Hebrews 12.3–13	**Evening Prayer** Psalms 56, 62 or **136** Jeremiah 22.20—23.8 John 12.1–11
Thursday	**21 March** Thomas Cranmer, archbishop, Reformation martyr, 1556 (see p.79)	*P(La)r*	Genesis 17.3–9 Psalm 105.4–9 John 8.51–end	Psalms 40, 125 or **143**, 146 Exodus 9.13–end Hebrews 12.14–end	Psalms 42, 43 or **138**, 140, 141 Jeremiah 23.9–32 John 12.12–19
Friday	**22 March**	*P(La)*	Jeremiah 20.10–13 Psalm 18.1–6 John 10.31–end	Psalms 22, 126 or 142, **144** Exodus 10 Hebrews 13.1–16	Psalm 31 or **145** Jeremiah 24 John 12.20–36a
Saturday	**23 March**	*P(La)*	Ezekiel 37.21–28 *Canticle:* Jeremiah 31.10–13 or Psalm 121 John 11.45–end	Psalms 23, 127 or **147** Exodus 11 Hebrews 13.17–end	Psalm 128, 129, **130** or **148**, 149, 150 Jeremiah 25.1–14 John 12.36b–end

Holy Week

		Principal Service	3rd Service	2nd Service
Sunday	**24 March** **Palm Sunday** R	Liturgy of the Palms: Mark 11.1–11 or John 12.12–16 Psalm 118.1–2,19–end [or 118.19–end] Liturgy of the Passion: Isaiah 50.4–9a Psalm 31.9–16 [or 31.9–18] Philippians 2.5–11 Mark 14.1—end of 15 or Mark 15.1–39 [40–end]	Psalms 61, 62 Zechariah 9.9–12 1 Corinthians 2.1–12	Psalm 69.1–20 Isaiah 5.1–7 Mark 12.1–12
		Holy Communion	**Morning Prayer**	**Evening Prayer**
			From the Monday of Holy Week until the Saturday of Easter Week the seasonal psalmody must be used.	
Monday	**25 March** **Monday of Holy Week** R	Isaiah 42.1–9 Psalm 36.5–11 Hebrews 9.11–15 John 12.1–11	Psalm 41 Lamentations 1.1–12a Luke 22.1–23	Psalm 25 Lamentations 2.8–19 Colossians 1.18–23
Tuesday	**26 March** **Tuesday of Holy Week** R	Isaiah 49.1–7 Psalm 71.1–14 [or 71.1–8] 1 Corinthians 1.18–31 John 12.20–36	Psalm 27 Lamentations 3.1–18 Luke 22.[24–38] 39–53	Psalm 55.13–24 Lamentations 3.40–51 Galatians 6.11–end
Wednesday	**27 March** **Wednesday of Holy Week** R	Isaiah 50.4–9a Psalm 70 Hebrews 12.1–3 John 13.21–32	Psalm 102 [or 102.1–18] Wisdom 1.16—2.1; [2.12–22] or Jeremiah 11.18–20 Luke 22.54–end	Psalm 88 Isaiah 63.1–9 Revelation 14.18—15.4
Thursday	**28 March** **Maundy Thursday** W	Exodus 12.1–4 [5–10] 11–14 Psalm 116.1, 10–end [or 116.9–end] 1 Corinthians 11.23–26 John 13.1–17, 31b–35	Psalms 42, 43 Leviticus 16.2–24 Luke 23.1–25	Psalm 39 Exodus 11 Ephesians 2.11–18
Friday	**29 March** **Good Friday** *Hangings removed; R for the Liturgy*	Isaiah 52.13—end of 53 Psalm 22 [or 22.1–11 or 22.1–21] Hebrews 10.16–25 or Hebrews 4.14–16; 5.7–9 John 18.1—end of 19	Psalm 69 Genesis 22.1–18 A part of John 18 and 19 may be read, if not used at the Principal Service or Hebrews 10.1–10	Psalms 130, 143 Lamentations 5.15–end John 19.38–end or Colossians 1.18–23

Easter

		Principal Service	3rd Service	2nd Service
Saturday	**30 March** **Easter Eve** *Hangings removed* *These readings are for use at services other than the Easter Vigil.*	Job 14.1–14 or Lamentations 3.1–9, 19–24 Psalm 31.1–4, 15–16 [or 31.1–5] 1 Peter 4.1–8 Matthew 27.57–end or John 19.38–end	Psalm 142 Hosea 6.1–6 John 2.18–22	Psalm 116 Job 19.21–27 1 John 5.5–12
Saturday **or Sunday**	**30 March evening** **31 March morning** *Easter Vigil* *The New Testament readings should be preceded by a minimum of three Old Testament readings.* *The Exodus reading should always be used.* *Gold or W*	Genesis 1.1—2.4a Genesis 7.1–5, 11–18; 8.6–18; 9.8–13 Genesis 22.1–18 **Exodus 14.10–end; 15.20–21** Isaiah 55.1–11 Baruch 3.9–15, 32—4.4 or Proverbs 8.1–8, 19–21; 9.4b–6 Ezekiel 36.24–28 Ezekiel 37.1–14 Zephaniah 3.14–end **Romans 6.3–11** **Mark 16.1–8**	Psalm 136.1–9, 23–end Psalm 46 Psalm 16 **Canticle: Exodus 15.1b–13, 17–18** *Canticle:* Isaiah 12.2–end Psalm 19 Psalms 42, 43 Psalm 143 Psalm 98 **Psalm 114**	
Sunday	**31 March** *Easter Day* *Gold or W*	Acts 10.34–43 † or Isaiah 25.6–9 Psalm 118.1–2, 14–24 [or 118.14–24] 1 Corinthians 15.1–11 or Acts 10.34–43 † John 20.1–18 or Mark 16.1–8 † *The reading from Acts must be used as either the first or second reading.*	*MP* Psalms 114, 117 Genesis 1.1–5, 26–end 2 Corinthians 5.14—6.2	*EP* Psalms 105 or 66.1–11 Ezekiel 37.1–14 Luke 24.13–35

			Holy Communion	Morning Prayer	Evening Prayer
Monday	**1 April** Monday of Easter Week	W	Acts 2.14, 22–32 Psalm 16.1–2, 6–end Matthew 28.8–15	Psalms **111**, 117, 146 Exodus 12.1–14 1 Corinthians 15.1–11	Psalm **135** Song of Solomon 1.9—2.7 Mark 16.1–8
Tuesday	**2 April** Tuesday of Easter Week	W	Acts 2.36–41 Psalm 33.4–5, 18–end John 20.11–18	Psalms **112**, 147.1–12 Exodus 12.14–36 1 Corinthians 15.12–19	Psalm **136** Song of Solomon 2.8–end Luke 24.1–12
Wednesday	**3 April** Wednesday of Easter Week	W	Acts 3.1–10 Psalm 105.1–9 Luke 24.13–35	Psalms **113**, 147.13–end Exodus 12.37–end 1 Corinthians 15.20–28	Psalm **105** Song of Solomon 3 Matthew 28.16–end
Thursday	**4 April** Thursday of Easter Week	W	Acts 3.11–end Psalm 8 Luke 24.35–48	Psalms **114**, 148 Exodus 13.1–16 1 Corinthians 15.29–34	Psalm **106** Song of Solomon 5.2—6.3 Luke 7.11–17
Friday	**5 April** Friday of Easter Week	W	Acts 4.1–12 Psalm 118.1–4, 22–26 John 21.1–14	Psalms **115**, 149 Exodus 13.17—14.14 1 Corinthians 15.35–50	Psalm **107** Song of Solomon 7.10—8.4 Luke 8.41–end
Saturday	**6 April** Saturday of Easter Week	W	Acts 4.13–21 Psalm 118.1–4, 14–21 Mark 16.9–15	Psalms **116**, 150 Exodus 14.15–end 1 Corinthians 15.51–end	Psalm **145** Song of Solomon 8.5–7 John 11.17–44

			Principal Service	3rd Service	2nd Service
Sunday	**7 April** **2nd Sunday of Easter**	W	[Exodus 14.10–end; 15.20–21] Acts 4.32–35 † Psalm 133 1 John 1.1—2.2 John 20.19–end † The reading from Acts must be used as either the first or second reading.	Psalm 22.20–31 Isaiah 53.6–12 Romans 4.13–25	1st **EP of the Annunciation** Psalm 85 Wisdom 9.1–12 or Genesis 3.8–15 Galatians 4.1–5
Monday	**8 April** Annunciation of Our Lord to the Blessed Virgin Mary (transferred from 25 March)	Gold or W	Isaiah 7.10–14 Psalm 40.5–11 Hebrews 10.4–10 Luke 1.26–38	MP Psalms 111, 113 1 Samuel 2.1–10 Romans 5.12–end	EP Psalms 131, 146 Isaiah 52.1–12 Hebrews 2.5–end
			Holy Communion	Morning Prayer	Evening Prayer
Tuesday	**9 April** Dietrich Bonhoeffer, Lutheran pastor, martyr, 1945	W	Acts 4.32–end Psalm 93 John 3.7–15	Psalms **8**, 20, 21 or **5**, 6 (8) Exodus 15.22—16.10 Colossians 1.15–end	Psalm 104 or 9, 10* Deuteronomy 1.19–40 John 20.11–18
Wednesday	**10 April** William Law, priest, spiritual writer, 1761 (see p.80) William of Ockham, friar, philosopher, teacher of the faith, 1347	W	Acts 5.17–26 Psalm 34.1–8 John 3.16–21	Psalms 16, **30** or 119.1–**32** Exodus 16.11–end Colossians 2.1–15	Psalm 33 or 11, 12, 13 Deuteronomy 3.18–end John 20.19–end
Thursday	**11 April** George Selwyn, bishop, 1878	W	Acts 5.27–33 Psalm 34.1, 15–end John 3.31–end	Psalms **28**, 29 or 14, **15**, 16 Exodus 17 Colossians 2.16—3.11	Psalm 34 or 18* Deuteronomy 4.1–14 John 21.1–14
Friday	**12 April**	W	Acts 5.34–42 Psalm 27.1–5, 16–17 John 6.1–15	Psalms 57, **61** or 17, **19** Exodus 18.1–12 Colossians 3.12—4.1	Psalm 118 or 22 Deuteronomy 4.15–31 John 21.15–19
Saturday	**13 April**	W	Acts 6.1–7 Psalm 33.1–5, 18–19 John 6.16–21	Psalms 63, **84** or 20, 21, **23** Exodus 18.13–end Colossians 4.2–end	Psalm 66 or 24, 25 Deuteronomy 4.32–40 John 21.20–end

Easter 3

		Principal Service	3rd Service	2nd Service
Sunday	**14 April** **3rd Sunday of Easter** W	[Zephaniah 3.14–end] Acts 3.12–19 † Psalm 4 1 John 3.1–7 Luke 24.36b–48 † *The reading from Acts must be used as either the first or second reading.*	Psalm 77.11–20 Isaiah 63.7–15 1 Corinthians 10.1–13	Psalm 142 Deuteronomy 7.7–13 Revelation 2.1–11 HC Luke 16.19–end

		Holy Communion	Morning Prayer	Evening Prayer
Monday	**15 April** W	Acts 6.8–15 Psalm 119.17–24 John 6.22–29	Psalms **96**, 97 or 27, **30** Exodus 19 Luke 1.1–25	Psalms **61**, 65 or 26, **28**, 29 Deuteronomy 5.1–22 Ephesians 1.1–14
Tuesday	**16 April** W *Isabella Gilmore, deaconess, 1923*	Acts 7.51—8.1a Psalm 31.1–5, 16 John 6.30–35	Psalms **98**, 99, 100 or 32, **36** Exodus 20.1–21 Luke 1.26–38	Psalm **71** or 33 Deuteronomy 5.22–end Ephesians 1.15–end
Wednesday	**17 April** W	Acts 8.1b–8 Psalm 66.1–6 John 6.35–40	Psalm **105** or 34 Exodus 24 Luke 1.39–56	Psalms 67, **72** or 119.**33–56** Deuteronomy 6 Ephesians 2.1–10
Thursday	**18 April** W	Acts 8.26–end Psalm 66.7–8, 14–end John 6.44–51	Psalm **136** or **37*** Exodus 25.1–22 Luke 1.57–end	Psalm **73** or 39, **40** Deuteronomy 7.1–11 Ephesians 2.11–end
Friday	**19 April** Wr Alphege, archbishop, martyr, 1012 (see p.79)	Acts 9.1–20 Psalm 117 John 6.52–59	Psalm **107** or 31 Exodus 28.1–4a, 29–38 Luke 2.1–20	Psalm **77** or 35 Deuteronomy 7.12–end Ephesians 3.1–13
Saturday	**20 April** W	Acts 9.31–42 Psalm 116.10–15 John 6.60–69	Psalms **108**, **110**, 111 or 41, **42**, 43 Exodus 29.1–9 Luke 2.21–40	Psalms 23, **27** or 45, **46** Deuteronomy 8 Ephesians 3.14–end

Easter 4

		Principal Service	3rd Service	2nd Service
Sunday 21 April 4th Sunday of Easter	W	**Holy Communion** [Genesis 7.1–5, 11–18; 8.6–18; 9.8–13] † Acts 4.5–12 † Psalm 23 1 John 3.16–end John 10.11–18 † *The reading from Acts must be used as either the first or second reading.*	**Morning Prayer** Psalm 119.89–96 Nehemiah 7.73b—8.12 Luke 24.25–32	**Evening Prayer** Psalm 81.8–16 Exodus 16.4–15 Revelation 2.12–17 HC John 6.30–40
Monday 22 April	W	**Holy Communion** Acts 11.1–18 Psalm 42.1–2; 43.1–4 John 10.1–10 (or 11–18)	**Morning Prayer** Psalm 103 or 44 Exodus 32.1–14 Luke 2.41–end	**Evening Prayer** Psalms 112, 113, **114** or **47, 49** Deuteronomy 9.1–21 Ephesians 4.1–16 or: 1st EP of George, martyr, patron of England: Psalms 111, 116; Jeremiah 15.15–end; Hebrews 11.32—12.2
Tuesday 23 April George, martyr, patron of England, c.304	R	**Principal Service** 1 Maccabees 2.59–64 or Revelation 12.7–12 Psalm 126 2 Timothy 2.3–13 John 15.18–21	**3rd Service** MP Psalms 5, 146 Joshua 1.1–9 Ephesians 6.10–20	**2nd Service** EP Psalms 3, 11 Isaiah 43.1–7 John 15.1–8
Wednesday 24 April Mellitus, bishop, 624 Seven Martyrs of the Melanesian Brotherhood, 2003	W	**Holy Communion** Acts 12.24—13.5 Psalm 67 John 12.44–end	**Morning Prayer** Psalm **135** or 119.57–80 Exodus 33 Luke 3.15–22	**Evening Prayer** Psalms 47, 48 or **59, 60** (67) Deuteronomy 10.12–end Ephesians 5.1–14 or: 1st EP of Mark the Evangelist: Psalm 19; Isaiah 52.7–10; Mark 1.1–15
Thursday 25 April Mark the Evangelist	R	**Principal Service** Proverbs 15.28–end or Acts 15.35–end Psalm 119.9–16 Ephesians 4.7–16 Mark 13.5–13	**3rd Service** MP Psalms 37.23–end, 148 Isaiah 62.6–10 or Ecclesiasticus 51.13–end Acts 12.25—13.13	**2nd Service** EP Psalm 45 Ezekiel 1.4–14 2 Timothy 4.1–11
Friday 26 April	W	**Holy Communion** Acts 13.26–33 Psalm 2 John 14.1–6	**Morning Prayer** Psalm 33 or 51, 54 Exodus 35.20—36.7 Luke 4.14–30	**Evening Prayer** Psalms 36, 40 or **38** Deuteronomy 12.1–14 Ephesians 6.1–9
Saturday 27 April Christina Rossetti, poet, 1894	W	**Holy Communion** Acts 13.44–end Psalm 98.1–5 John 14.7–14	**Morning Prayer** Psalm 34 or **68** Exodus 40.17–end Luke 4.31–37	**Evening Prayer** Psalms 84, 86 or 65, **66** Deuteronomy 15.1–18 Ephesians 6.10–end

Easter 5

	Principal Service	3rd Service	2nd Service
Sunday 28 April **5th Sunday of Easter** W	[Baruch 3.9–15, 32—4.4 or Genesis 22.1–18] Acts 8.26–end † Psalm 22.25–end 1 John 4.7–end John 15.1–8 † *The reading from Acts must be used as either the first or second reading.*	Psalm 44.16–end 2 Maccabees 7.7–14 or Daniel 3.16–28 Hebrews 11.32—12.2	Psalm 96 Isaiah 60.1–14 Revelation 3.1–13 HC Mark 16.9–16

	Holy Communion	Morning Prayer	Evening Prayer
Monday 29 April Catherine of Siena, teacher of the faith, 1380 (see p.80) W	Acts 14.5–18 Psalm 118.1–3, 14–15 John 14.21–26	Psalm 145 or 71 Numbers 9.15–end; 10.33–end Luke 4.38–end	Psalm 105 or 72, 75 Deuteronomy 16.1–20 1 Peter 1.1–12
Tuesday 30 April *Pandita Mary Ramabai, translator, 1922* W	Acts 14.19–end Psalm 145.10–end John 14.27–end	Psalms 19, 147.1–12 or 73 Numbers 11.1–33 Luke 5.1–11	Psalms 96, 97, 74 Deuteronomy 17.8–end 1 Peter 1.13–end *or:* 1st EP of Philip and James, Apostles: Psalm 25; Isaiah 40.27–end; John 12.20–26

	Principal Service	3rd Service	2nd Service
Wednesday 1 May Philip and James, Apostles R	Isaiah 30.15–21 Psalm 119.1–8 Ephesians 1.3–10 John 14.1–14	MP Psalms 139, 146 Proverbs 4.10–18 James 1.1–12	EP Psalm 149 Job 23.1–12 John 1.43–end

	Holy Communion	Morning Prayer	Evening Prayer
Thursday 2 May Athanasius, bishop, teacher of the faith, 373 (see p.80) W	Acts 15.7–21 Psalm 96.1–3, 7–10 John 15.9–11	Psalms 57, 148 or 78.1–39* Numbers 13.1–3, 17–end Luke 5.27–end	Psalm 104 or 78.40–end* Deuteronomy 19 1 Peter 2.11–end
Friday 3 May W	Acts 15.22–31 Psalm 57.8–end John 15.12–17	Psalms 138, 149 or 55 Numbers 14.1–25 Luke 6.1–11	Psalm 66 or 69 Deuteronomy 21.22—22.8 1 Peter 3.1–12
Saturday 4 May English saints and martyrs of the Reformation Era W	Acts 16.1–10 Psalm 100 John 15.18–21 *Lesser Festival eucharistic lectionary:* Isaiah 43.1–7 or Ecclesiasticus 2.10–17 Psalm 87 2 Corinthians 4.5–12 John 12.20–26	Psalms 146, 150 or 76, 79 Numbers 14.26–end Luke 6.12–26	Psalm 118, 81, 84 Deuteronomy 24.5–end 1 Peter 3.13–end

		Principal Service	3rd Service	2nd Service
Sunday	**5 May** W **6th Sunday of Easter**	[Isaiah 55.1–11] Acts 10.44–end † Psalm 98 1 John 5.1–6 John 15.9–17 † *The reading from Acts must be used as either the first or second reading.*	Psalm 104.26–32 Ezekiel 47.1–12 John 21.1–19	Psalm 45 Song of Solomon 4.16—5.2; 8.6.7 Revelation 3.14–end HC Luke 22.24–30

		Holy Communion	Morning Prayer	Evening Prayer
Monday	**6 May** W Rogation Day	Acts 16.11–15 Psalm 149.1–5 John 15.26—16.4	Psalms 65, 67 or **80, 82** Numbers 16.1–35 Luke 6.27–38	Psalms **121**, 122, 123 or **85, 86** Deuteronomy 26 1 Peter 4.1–11
Tuesday	**7 May** W Rogation Day	Acts 16.22–34 Psalm 138 John 16.5–11	Psalms 124, 125, **126**, 127 or 87, **89.1–18** Numbers 16.36–end Luke 6.39–end	Psalms **128**, 129, 130, 131 or **89.19–end** Deuteronomy 28.1–14 1 Peter 4.12–end
Wednesday	**8 May** W Julian of Norwich, spiritual writer, c.1417 (see p.82) Rogation Day	Acts 17.15, 22—18.1 Psalm 148.1–2, 11–end John 16.12–15	Psalms **132**, 133 or **119.105–128** Numbers 17.1–11 Luke 7.1–10 Colossians 2.20—3.4	1st EP of Ascension Day Psalms 15, 24 2 Samuel 23.1–5

		Principal Service	3rd Service	2nd Service
Thursday	**9 May** Gold or W **Ascension Day**	Acts 1.1–11 † or Daniel 7.9–14 Psalm 47 or Psalm 93 Ephesians 1.15–end or Acts 1.1–11 † Luke 24.44–end † *The reading from Acts must be used as either the first or second reading.*	MP Psalms 110, 150 Isaiah 52.7–end Hebrews 7.[1–25] 26–end	EP Psalm 8 Song of the Three 29–37 or 2 Kings 2.1–15 Revelation 5 HC Matthew 28.16–end

The nine days after Ascension Day until the eve of Pentecost are observed as days of prayer and preparation for the celebration of the outpouring of the Holy Spirit.
From 10–18 May, in preparation for the Day of Pentecost, an alternative sequence of daily readings for use at the one of the offices is marked with an asterisk *.

		Holy Communion	Morning Prayer	Evening Prayer
Friday	**10 May** W	Acts 18.9–18 Psalm 47.1–6 John 16.20–23	Psalms 20, **81** or 88 (95) Numbers 20.1–13 Luke 7.11–17 *Exodus 35.30—36.1; Galatians 5.13–end*	Psalm **145** or **102** Deuteronomy 29.2–15 1 John 1.1—2.6
Saturday	**11 May** W	Acts 18.22–end Psalm 47.1–2, 7–end John 16.23–28	Psalms 21, **47** or 96, **97**, 100 Numbers 21.4–9 Luke 7.18–35 *Numbers 11.16–17, 24–29; 1 Corinthians 2*	Psalms 84, **85** or **104** Deuteronomy 30 1 John 2.7–17

Easter 7

	Principal Service	3rd Service	2nd Service
Sunday 12 May W **7th Sunday of Easter** *Sunday after Ascension Day*	[Ezekiel 36.24–28] Acts 1.15–17, 21–end † Psalm 1 1 John 5.9–13 John 17.6–19 † *The reading from Acts must be used as either the first or second reading.*	Psalm 76 Isaiah 14.3–15 Revelation 14.1–13	Psalm 147.1–12 Isaiah 61 Luke 4.14–21

	Holy Communion	Morning Prayer	Evening Prayer
Monday 13 May W	Acts 19.1–8 Psalm 68.1–6 John 16.29–end	Psalms **93**, 96, **97** or **98**, 99, 101 Numbers 22.1–35 Luke 7.36–end * *Numbers 27.15–end;* *1 Corinthians 3*	Psalm 18 or **105*** *(or 103)* Deuteronomy 31.1–13 1 John 2.18–end *or:* 1st EP of Matthias the Apostle: Psalm 147; Isaiah 22.15–22; Philippians 3.13b–4.1

	Principal Service	3rd Service	2nd Service
Tuesday 14 May R *Matthias the Apostle*	Isaiah 22.15–end or Acts 1.15–end Psalm 15 Acts 1.15–end or 1 Corinthians 4.1–7 John 15.9–17	MP Psalms 16, 147.1–12 1 Samuel 2.27–35 Acts 2.37–end	EP Psalm 80 1 Samuel 16.1–13a Matthew 7.15–27

	Holy Communion	Morning Prayer	Evening Prayer
Wednesday 15 May W	Acts 20.28–end Psalm 68.27–28, 32–end John 17.11–19	Psalms 2, **29** or 110, **111**, 112 Numbers 23.13–end Luke 8.16–25 **1 Kings 19.1–18; Matthew 3.13–end*	Psalms 36, **46** or 119.129–**152** Deuteronomy 31.30—32.14 1 John 3.11–end
Thursday 16 May W *Caroline Chisholm, social reformer, 1877*	Acts 22.30; 23.6–11 Psalm 16.1, 5–end John 17.20–end	Psalms **24**, 72 or 113, **115** Numbers 24 Luke 8.26–39 **Ezekiel 11.14–20; Matthew 9.35—10.20*	Psalm 139 or 114, **116**, 117 Deuteronomy 32.15–47 1 John 4.1–6
Friday 17 May W	Acts 25.13–21 Psalm 103.1–2, 11–12, 19–20 John 21.15–19	Psalms 28, 30 or **139** Numbers 27.12–end Luke 8.40–end **Ezekiel 36.22–28; Matthew 12.22–32*	Psalm **147** or 130, **131**, 137 Deuteronomy 33 1 John 4.7–end
Saturday 18 May W	Acts 28.16–20, 30–end Psalm 11.4–end John 21.20–end	Psalms 42, **43** or 120, **121**, 122 Numbers 32.1–27 Luke 9.1–17 **Micah 3.1–8;* *Ephesians 6.10–20 (at MP only)*	**1st EP of Pentecost** Psalm 48 Deuteronomy 16.9–15 John 7.37–39

		Principal Service	3rd Service	2nd Service
Sunday 19 May Pentecost Whit Sunday	R	Acts 2.1–21 † or Ezekiel 37.1–14 Psalm 104.26–36,37b [or 104.26–end] Romans 8.22–27 or Acts 2.1–21 † John 15.26–27; 16.4b–15 † The reading from Acts must be used as either the first or second reading.	MP Psalm 145 Isaiah 11.1–9 or Wisdom 7.15–23 [24–27] 1 Corinthians 12.4–13	EP Psalm 139.1–11 [13–18, 23–24] Ezekiel 36.22–28 Acts 2.22–38 HC John 20.19–23
		Holy Communion	Morning Prayer	Evening Prayer
Monday 20 May Alcuin, deacon, abbot, 804 (see p.82) Ordinary Time resumes today DEL week 7	Gw	James 3.13–end Psalm 19.7–end Mark 9.14–29	Psalms 123, 124, 125, **126** Joshua 1 Luke 9.18–27	Psalms **127**, 128, 129 Job 1 Romans 1.1–17
Tuesday 21 May Helena, protector of the Holy Places, 330	G	James 4.1–10 Psalm 55.7–9, 24 Mark 9.30–37	Psalms **132**, 133 Joshua 2 Luke 9.28–36	Psalms (134,) **135** Job 2 Romans 1.18–end
Wednesday 22 May	G	James 4.13–end Psalm 49.1–2, 5–10 Mark 9.38–40	Psalm 119.153–end Joshua 3 Luke 9.37–50	Psalm 136 Job 3 Romans 2.1–16
Thursday 23 May	G	James 5.1–6 Psalm 49.12–20 Mark 9.41–50	Psalms **143**, 146 Joshua 4.1—5.1 Luke 9.51–end	Psalms **138**, 140, 141 Job 4 Romans 2.17–end
Friday 24 May John and Charles Wesley, evangelists, hymn writers, 1791 and 1788 (see p.81)	Gw	James 5.9–12 Psalm 103.1–4, 8–13 Mark 10.1–12	Psalms 142, **144** Joshua 5.2–end Luke 10.1–16	Psalm 145 Job 5 Romans 3.1–20
Saturday 25 May The Venerable Bede, monk, scholar, historian, 735 (see p.82) Aldhelm, bishop, 709	Gw	James 5.13–end Psalm 141.1–4 Mark 10.13–16	Psalm 147 Joshua 6.1–20 Luke 10.17–24	**1st EP of Trinity Sunday** Psalms 97, 98 Isaiah 40.12–end Mark 1.1–13

Trinity Sunday

		Principal Service	3rd Service	2nd Service
Sunday 26 May Trinity Sunday	Gold or W	**Holy Communion** Isaiah 6.1–8 Psalm 29 Romans 8.12–17 John 3.1–17	**Morning Prayer** *MP* Psalm 33.1–12 Proverbs 8.1–4, 22–31 2 Corinthians 13.[5–10] 11–end	**Evening Prayer** *EP* Psalm 104.1–10 Ezekiel 1.4–10, 22–28a Revelation 4 *HC* Mark 1.1–13
Monday 27 May DEL week 8	G	1 Peter 1.3–9 Psalm 111 Mark 10.17–27	Psalms 1, 2, 3 Joshua 7.1–15 Luke 10.25–37	Psalms 4, 7 Job 7 Romans 4.1–12
Tuesday 28 May *Lanfranc, monk, archbishop, scholar, 1089*	G	1 Peter 1.10–16 Psalm 98.1–5 Mark 10.28–31	Psalms 5, 6 (8) Joshua 7.16–end Luke 10.38–end	Psalms 9, 10* Job 8 Romans 4.13–end

If Corpus Christi is kept as a Festival:

		Principal Service	3rd Service	2nd Service
Wednesday 29 May	G	1 Peter 1.18–end Psalm 147.13–end Mark 10.32–45	Psalm 119.1–32 Joshua 8.1–29 Luke 11.1–13	Psalms 11, 12, 13 Job 9 Romans 5.1–11 or: 1st EP of Corpus Christi: Psalms 110, 111; Exodus 16.2–15; John 6.22–35
Thursday 30 May Day of Thanksgiving for the Institution of Holy Communion (Corpus Christi)	W	**Principal Service** Genesis 14.18–20 Psalm 116.10–end 1 Corinthians 11.23–26 John 6.51–58	**3rd Service** *MP* Psalm 147 Deuteronomy 8.2–16 1 Corinthians 10.1–17	**2nd Service** *EP* Psalms 23, 42, 43 Proverbs 9.1–5 Luke 9.11–17
Friday 31 May Visit of the Blessed Virgin Mary to Elizabeth	W	Zephaniah 3.14–18 Psalm 113 Romans 12.9–16 Luke 1.39–49 [50–56]	*MP* Psalms 85, 150 1 Samuel 2.1–10 Mark 3.31–end	*EP* Psalms 122, 127, 128 Zechariah 2.10–end John 3.25–30
Saturday 1 June *Justin, martyr, c.165* (see p.79)	Gr	**Holy Communion** Jude 17, 20–end Psalm 63.1–6 Mark 11.27–end	**Morning Prayer** Psalms 20, 21, 23 Joshua 10.1–15 Luke 11.37–end	**Evening Prayer** Psalms 24, 25 Job 12 Romans 6.15–end

Trinity Sunday

If Corpus Christi is not kept as a Festival:

	Holy Communion	Morning Prayer	Evening Prayer
Wednesday 29 May G	1 Peter 1.18–end Psalm 147.13–end Mark 10.32–45	Psalm 119.1–32 Joshua 8.1–29 Luke 11.1–13	Psalms 11, 12, 13 Job 9 Romans 5.1–11
Thursday 30 May Gw Josephine Butler, social reformer, 1906 (see p.83) Joan of Arc, visionary, 1431 Apolo Kivebulaya, priest, evangelist, 1933	1 Peter 2.2–5, 9–12 Psalm 100 Mark 10.46–end	Psalms 14, **15**, 16 Joshua 8.30–end Luke 11.14–28	Psalm 18* Job 10 Romans 5.12–end or: 1st EP of the Visit of the BVM to Elizabeth: Psalm 45; Song of Solomon 2.8–14; Luke 1.26–38

	Principal Service	3rd Service	2nd Service
Friday 31 May W Visit of the Blessed Virgin Mary to Elizabeth	Zephaniah 3.14–18 Psalm 113 Romans 12.9–16 Luke 1.39–49 [50–56]	MP Psalms 85, 150 1 Samuel 2.1–10 Mark 3.31–end	EP Psalms 122, 127, 128 Zechariah 2.10–end John 3.25–30

	Holy Communion	Morning Prayer	Evening Prayer
Saturday 1 June Gr Justin, martyr, c.165 (see p.79)	Jude 17, 20–end Psalm 63.1–6 Mark 11.27–end	Psalms 20, 21, **23** Joshua 10.1–15 Luke 11.37–end	Psalms **24**, 25 Job 12 Romans 6.15–end

Trinity 1

		Principal Service		3rd Service	2nd Service
Sunday	**2 June** 1st Sunday after Trinity Proper 4	G	*Continuous:* 1 Samuel 3.1–10 [11–20] Psalm 139.1–5, 12–18	*Related:* Deuteronomy 5.12–15 Psalm 81.1–10 2 Corinthians 4.5–12 Mark 2.23—3.6	Psalms 28, 32 Deuteronomy 5.1–21 Acts 21.17–39a	Psalm 35 [or 35.1–10] Jeremiah 5.1–19 Romans 7.7–end HC Luke 7.1–10
			Holy Communion		**Morning Prayer**	**Evening Prayer**
Monday	**3 June** *Martyrs of Uganda, 1885–7, 1977* DEL week 9	G	2 Peter 1.2–7 Psalm 91.1–2, 14–end Mark 12.1–12		Psalms 27, **30** Joshua 14 Luke 12.1–12	Psalms 26, **28**, 29 Job 13 Romans 7.1–6
Tuesday	**4 June** *Petroc, abbot, 6th cent.*	G	2 Peter 3.11–15a, 17–end Psalm 90.1–4, 10, 14, 16 Mark 12.13–17		Psalms 32, **36** Joshua 21.43—22.8 Luke 12.13–21	Psalm **33** Job 14 Romans 7.7–end
Wednesday	**5 June** *Boniface (Wynfrith), bishop,* *martyr, 754 (see p.79)*	Gr	2 Timothy 1.1–3, 6–12 Psalm 123 Mark 12.18–27		Psalm **34** Joshua 22.9–end Luke 12.22–31	Psalm 1**19.33–56** Job 15 Romans 8.1–11
Thursday	**6 June** *Ini Kopuria, founder of the* *Melanesian Brotherhood, 1945*	G	2 Timothy 2.8–15 Psalm 25.4–12 Mark 12.28–34		Psalm **37*** Joshua 23 Luke 12.32–40	Psalms 39, **40** Job 16.1—17.2 Romans 8.12–17
Friday	**7 June**	G	2 Timothy 3.10–end Psalm 119.161–168 Mark 12.35–37		Psalm **31** Joshua 24.1–28 Luke 12.41–48	Psalm **35** Job 17.3–end Romans 8.18–30
Saturday	**8 June** *Thomas Ken, bishop, nonjuror,* *hymn writer, 1711 (see p.81)*	Gw	2 Timothy 4.1–8 Psalm 71.7–16 Mark 12.38–end		Psalms 41, **42**, 43 Joshua 24.29–end Luke 12.49–end	Psalms 45, **46** Job 18 Romans 8.31–end

Trinity 2

		Principal Service		3rd Service	2nd Service
Sunday	**9 June** G **2nd Sunday after Trinity** Proper 5	*Continuous:* 1 Samuel 8.4–11 [12–15] 16–20; [11.14–end] Psalm 138	*Related:* Genesis 3.8–15 Psalm 130 2 Corinthians 4.13—5.1 Mark 3.20–end	Psalm 36 Deuteronomy 6.10–end Acts 22.22—23.11	Psalm 37.1–11 [12–17] Jeremiah 6.16–21 Romans 9.1–13 HC Luke 7.11–17
		Holy Communion		Morning Prayer	Evening Prayer
Monday	**10 June** G DEL week 10	1 Kings 17.1–6 Psalm 121 Matthew 5.1–12		Psalm **44** Judges 2 Luke 13.1–9	Psalms **47, 49** Job 19 Romans 9.1–18 or: 1st EP of Barnabas the Apostle: Psalms 1, 15; Isaiah 42.5–12; Acts 14.8–end
		Principal Service		3rd Service	2nd Service
Tuesday	**11 June** R Barnabas the Apostle	Job 29.11–16 or Acts 11.19–end Psalm 112 Acts 11.19–end or Galatians 2.1–10 John 15.12–17		MP Psalms 100, 101, 117 Jeremiah 9.23–24 Acts 4.32–end	EP Psalm 147 Ecclesiastes 12.9–end or Tobit 4.5–11 Acts 9.26–31
		Holy Communion		Morning Prayer	Evening Prayer
Wednesday	**12 June** G	1 Kings 18.20–39 Psalm 16.1, 6–end Matthew 5.17–19		Psalm 119.57–**80** Judges 5 Luke 13.22–end	Psalms **59, 60** (67) Job 22 Romans 10.1–10
Thursday	**13 June** G	1 Kings 18.41–end Psalm 65.8–end Matthew 5.20–26		Psalms 56, **57** (63*) Judges 6.1–24 Luke 14.1–11	Psalms 61, **62, 64** Job 23 Romans 10.11–end
Friday	**14 June** G *Richard Baxter, puritan divine, 1691*	1 Kings 19.9, 11–16 Psalm 27.8–16 Matthew 5.27–32		Psalms **51, 54** Judges 6.25–end Luke 14.12–24	Psalm **38** Job 24 Romans 11.1–12
Saturday	**15 June** G *Evelyn Underhill, spiritual writer, 1941*	1 Kings 19.19–end Psalm 16.1–7 Matthew 5.33–37		Psalm **68** Judges 7 Luke 14.25–end	Psalms 65, **66** Job 25–26 Romans 11.13–24

Trinity 3

		Principal Service		3rd Service	2nd Service
Sunday	**16 June** **3rd Sunday after Trinity** Proper 6	G	*Continuous:* 1 Samuel 15.34—16.13 Psalm 20	*Related:* Ezekiel 17.22–end Psalm 92.1–4,12–end [or 92.1–8] 2 Corinthians 5.6–10 [11–13] 14–17 Mark 4.26–34	Psalms 42, 43 Deuteronomy 10.12—11.1 Acts 23.12–35	Psalm 39 Jeremiah 7.1–16 Romans 9.14–26 *HC* Luke 7.36—8.3
			Holy Communion		Morning Prayer	Evening Prayer
Monday	**17 June** *Samuel and Henrietta Barnett, social reformers, 1913 and 1936* DEL week 11	G	1 Kings 21.1–16 Psalm 5.1–5 Matthew 5.38–42		Psalm 71 Judges 8.22–end Luke 15.1–10	Psalms 72, 75 Job 27 Romans 11.25–end
Tuesday	**18 June** *Bernard Mizeki, martyr, 1896*	G	1 Kings 21.17–end Psalm 51.1–9 Matthew 5.43–end		Psalm 73 Judges 9.1–21 Luke 15.11–end	Psalm 74 Job 28 Romans 12.1–8
Wednesday	**19 June** *Sundar Singh, sadhu (holy man), evangelist, teacher of the faith, 1929*	G	2 Kings 2.1, 6–14 Psalm 31.21–end Matthew 6.1–6, 16–18		Psalm 77 Judges 9.22–end Luke 16.1–18	Psalm 119.81–104 Job 29 Romans 12.9–end
Thursday	**20 June**	G	Ecclesiasticus 48.1–14 or Isaiah 63.7–9 Psalm 97.1–8 Matthew 6.7–15		Psalm 78.1–39* Judges 11.1–11 Luke 16.19–end	Psalm 78.40–end* Job 30 Romans 13.1–7
Friday	**21 June**	G	2 Kings 11.1–4, 9–18, 20 Psalm 132.1–5, 11–13 Matthew 6.19–23		Psalm 55 Judges 11.29–end Luke 17.1–10	Psalm 69 Job 31 Romans 13.8–end
Saturday	**22 June** *Alban, first martyr of Britain, c.250* (see p.79)	Gr	2 Chronicles 24.17–25 Psalm 89.25–33 Matthew 6.24–end		Psalms 76, 79 Judges 12.1–7 Luke 17.11–19	Psalms 81, 84 Job 32 Romans 14.1–12

		Principal Service	3rd Service	2nd Service
Sunday	**23 June** **4th Sunday after Trinity** Proper 7 — *G*	*Continuous:* 1 Samuel 17.[1a, 4–11, 19–23] 32–49 Psalm 9.9–end or 1 Samuel 17.57–18.5, 10–16 Psalm 133 — *Related:* Job 38.1–11 Psalm 107.1–3, 23–32 [or 107.23–32] — 2 Corinthians 6.1–13 Mark 4.35–end	Psalm 48 Deuteronomy 11.1–15 Acts 27.1–12	Psalm 49 Jeremiah 10.1–16 Romans 11.25–end HC Luke 8.26–39 or: 1st EP of the Birth of John the Baptist: Psalm 71; Judges 13.2–7, 24–end; Luke 1.5–25
Monday	**24 June** Birth of John the Baptist — *W*	**Holy Communion** Isaiah 40.1–11 Psalm 85.7–end Acts 13.14b–26 or Galatians 3.23–end Luke 1.57–66, 80	**Morning Prayer** MP Psalms 50, 149 Ecclesiasticus 48.1–10 or Malachi 3.1–6 Luke 3.1–17	**Evening Prayer** EP Psalms 80, 82 Malachi 4 Matthew 11.2–19
Tuesday	**25 June** DEL week 12 — *G*	2 Kings 19.9b–11, 14–21, 31–36 Psalm 48.1–2, 8–end Matthew 7.6, 12–14	Psalms 87, 89.1–18 Judges 14 Luke 18.1–14	Psalm 89.19–end Job 38 Romans 15.1–13
Wednesday	**26 June** Ember Day — *G*	2 Kings 22.8–13; 23.1–3 Psalm 119.33–40 Matthew 7.15–20	Psalm 119.105–128 Judges 15.1—16.3 Luke 18.15–30	Psalms 91, 93 Job 39 Romans 15.14–21
Thursday	**27 June** *Cyril, bishop, teacher of the faith, 444* — *G*	2 Kings 24.8–17 Psalm 79.1–9, 12 Matthew 7.21–end	Psalms 90, 92 Judges 16.4–end Luke 18.31–end	Psalm 94 Job 40 Romans 15.22–end
Friday	**28 June** *Irenaeus, bishop, teacher of the faith, c.200* (see p.80) Ember Day — *Gw*	2 Kings 25.1–12 Psalm 137.1–6 Matthew 8.1–4	Psalms 88 (95) Judges 17 Luke 19.1–10	Psalm 102 Job 41 Romans 16.1–16 or: 1st EP of Peter and Paul, Apostles [or †Peter the Apostle alone]: Psalms 66, 67; Ezekiel 3.4–11; Galatians 1.13—2.8 [†Acts 9.32–end]
Saturday	**29 June** Peter and Paul, Apostles *or* Peter the Apostle Ember Day — *R*	**Principal Service** Peter and Paul: Zechariah 4.1–6a, 10b–end or Acts 12.1–11 Psalm 125 Acts 12.1–11 or 2 Timothy 4.6–8, 17–18 Matthew 16.13–19 — Peter alone: Ezekiel 3.22–end or Acts 12.1–11 Psalm 125 Acts 12.1–11 or 1 Peter 2.19–end Matthew 16.13–19	**3rd Service** MP Psalms 71, 113 Isaiah 49.1–6 Acts 11.1–18	**2nd Service** EP Psalms 124, 138 Ezekiel 34.11–16 John 21.15–22

		Principal Service		3rd Service	2nd Service
Sunday	**30 June** G **5th Sunday after Trinity** Proper 8	*Continuous:* 2 Samuel 1.1, 17–end Psalm 130	*Related:* Wisdom 1.13–15; 2.23–24 *Canticle:* Lamentations 3.23–33 or Psalm 30 † *Lamentations 3.23–33 may be read as the first reading in place of Wisdom 1.13–15; 2.23–24* 2 Corinthians 8.7–end Mark 5.21–end	Psalm 56 Deuteronomy 15.1–11 Acts 27.[13–32] 33–end	Psalms [52] 53 Jeremiah 11.1–14 Romans 13.1–10 HC Luke 9.51–end
		Holy Communion		**Morning Prayer**	**Evening Prayer**
Monday	**1 July** G *Henry, John, and Henry Venn, priests, evangelical divines, 1797, 1813, 1873* DEL week 13	Amos 2.6–10, 13–end Psalm 50.16–23 Matthew 8.18–22		Psalms **98**, 99, 101 1 Samuel 1.1–20 Luke 19.28–40	Psalm **105*** (or 103) Ezekiel 1.1–14 2 Corinthians 1.1–14
Tuesday	**2 July** G	Amos 3.1–8, 4.11–12 Psalm 5.8–end Matthew 8.23–27		Psalm **106*** (or 103) 1 Samuel 1.21—2.11 Luke 19.41–end	Psalm **107*** Ezekiel 1.15—2.2 2 Corinthians 1.15—2.4 or: 1st EP of Thomas the Apostle: Psalm 27; Isaiah 35; Hebrews 10.35—11.1
		Principal Service		**3rd Service**	**2nd Service**
Wednesday	**3 July** R Thomas the Apostle	Habakkuk 2.1–4 Psalm 31.1–6 Ephesians 2.19–end John 20.24–29		MP Psalms 92, 146 2 Samuel 15.17–21 or Ecclesiasticus 2 John 11.1–16	EP Psalm 139 Job 42.1–6 1 Peter 1.3–12
		Holy Communion		**Morning Prayer**	**Evening Prayer**
Thursday	**4 July** G	Amos 7.10–end Psalm 19.7–10 Matthew 9.1–8		Psalms 113, **115** 1 Samuel 2.27–end Luke 20.9–19	Psalms 114, **116**, 117 Ezekiel 3.12–end 2 Corinthians 3
Friday	**5 July** G	Amos 8.4–6, 9–12 Psalm 119.1–8 Matthew 9.9–13		Psalm **139** 1 Samuel 3.1—4.1*a* Luke 20.20–26	Psalms **130**, 131, 137 Ezekiel 8 2 Corinthians 4
Saturday	**6 July** G *Thomas More, scholar, and John Fisher, bishop, martyrs, 1535*	Amos 9.11–end Psalm 85.8–end Matthew 9.14–17		Psalms 120, **121**, 122 1 Samuel 4.1*b*–end Luke 20.27–40	Psalm **118** Ezekiel 9 2 Corinthians 5

		Principal Service		3rd Service	2nd Service
Sunday	7 July 6th Sunday after Trinity Proper 9	G	*Continuous:* 2 Samuel 5.1–5, 9–10 Psalm 48	*Related:* Ezekiel 2.1–5 Psalm 123 2 Corinthians 12.2–10 Mark 6.1–13	Psalm 57 Deuteronomy 24.10–end Acts 28.1–16	Psalms [63] 64 Jeremiah 20.1–11a Romans 14.1–17 HC Luke 10.1–11, 16–20
			Holy Communion		Morning Prayer	Evening Prayer
Monday	8 July DEL week 14	G	Hosea 2.14–16, 19–20 Psalm 145.2–9 Matthew 9.18–26		Psalms 123, 124, 125, 126 1 Samuel 5 Luke 20.41—21.4	Psalms 127, 128, 129 Ezekiel 10.1–19 2 Corinthians 6.1—7.1
Tuesday	9 July	G	Hosea 8.4–7, 11–13 Psalm 103.8–12 Matthew 9.32–end		Psalms 132, 133 1 Samuel 6.1–16 Luke 21.5–19	Psalms (134,) 135 Ezekiel 11.14–end 2 Corinthians 7.2–end
Wednesday	10 July	G	Hosea 10.1–3, 7–8, 12 Psalm 115.3–10 Matthew 10.1–7		Psalm 119.153–end 1 Samuel 7 Luke 21.20–28	Psalm 136 Ezekiel 12.1–16 2 Corinthians 8.1–15
Thursday	11 July Benedict, abbot, c.550 (see p.82)	Gw	Hosea 11.1, 3–4, 8–9 Psalm 105.1–7 Matthew 10.7–15		Psalms 143, 146 1 Samuel 8 Luke 21.29–end	Psalms 138, 140, 141 Ezekiel 12.17–end 2 Corinthians 8.16—9.5
Friday	12 July	G	Hosea 14.2–end Psalm 80.1–7 Matthew 10.16–23		Psalms 142, 144 1 Samuel 9.1–14 Luke 22.1–13	Psalm 145 Ezekiel 13.1–16 2 Corinthians 9.6–end
Saturday	13 July	G	Isaiah 6.1–8 Psalm 51.1–7 Matthew 10.24–33		Psalm 147 1 Samuel 9.15—10.1 Luke 22.14–23	Psalms 148, 149, 150 Ezekiel 14.1–11 2 Corinthians 10

Trinity 7

		Principal Service		3rd Service	2nd Service
Sunday	**14 July** G **7th Sunday after Trinity** Proper 10	*Continuous:* 2 Samuel 6.1–5, 12b–19 Psalm 24	*Related:* Amos 7.7–15 Psalm 85.8–end	Psalm 65 Deuteronomy 28.1–14 Acts 28.17–end	Psalm 66 [or 66.1–8] Job 4.1; 5.6–end or Ecclesiasticus 4.11–end Romans 15.14–29 HC Luke 10.25–37
			Ephesians 1.3–14 Mark 6.14–29		
		Holy Communion		Morning Prayer	Evening Prayer
Monday	**15 July** Gw Swithun, bishop, c.862 (see p.81) *Bonaventure, friar, bishop,* *teacher of the faith, 1274* DEL week 15	Isaiah 1.11–17 Psalm 50.7–15 Matthew 10.34—11.1		Psalms **1**, 2, **3** 1 Samuel 10.1–16 Luke 22.24–30	Psalms **4**, **7** Ezekiel 14.12–end 2 Corinthians 11.1–15
Tuesday	**16 July** G *Osmund, bishop, 1099*	Isaiah 7.1–9 Psalm 48.1–7 Matthew 11.20–24		Psalms **5**, 6 (8) 1 Samuel 10.17–end Luke 22.31–38	Psalms **9**, 10* Ezekiel 18.1–20 2 Corinthians 11.16–end
Wednesday	**17 July** G	Isaiah 10.5–7, 13–16 Psalm 94.5–11 Matthew 11.25–27		Psalm 1**19**.1–**32** 1 Samuel 11 Luke 22.39–46	Psalms **11**, 12, 13 Ezekiel 18.21–32 2 Corinthians 12
Thursday	**18 July** G *Elizabeth Ferard, deaconess, founder of the* *Community of St Andrew, 1883*	Isaiah 26.7–9, 16–19 Psalm 102.14–21 Matthew 11.28–end		Psalms 14, **15**, 16 1 Samuel 12 Luke 22.47–62	Psalm 1**8** Ezekiel 20.1–20 2 Corinthians 13
Friday	**19 July** Gw Gregory, bishop, and his sister Macrina, deaconess, teachers of the faith, c.394 and c.379 (see p.80)	Isaiah 38.1–6, 21–22, 7–8 [sic] *Canticle:* Isaiah 38.10–16 or Psalm 32.1–8 Matthew 12.1–8		Psalms 17, 1**9** 1 Samuel 13.5–18 Luke 22.63–end	Psalm **22** Ezekiel 20.21–38 James 1.1–11
Saturday	**20 July** G *Margaret of Antioch, martyr, 4th cent.* *Bartolomé de las Casas,* *Apostle to the Indies, 1566*	Micah 2.1–5 Psalm 10.1–5a, 12 Matthew 12.14–21		Psalms 20, 21, **23** 1 Samuel 19.1–18 Luke 23.1–12	Psalms **24**, **25** Ezekiel 24.15–end James 1.12–end

47

		Principal Service	3rd Service	2nd Service
Sunday	G	*Continuous:* *Related:*	Psalms 67, 70	Psalm 73 [or 73.21–end]
21 July		2 Samuel 7.1–14a Jeremiah 23.1–6	Deuteronomy 30.1–10	Job 13.13—14.6
8th Sunday after Trinity		Psalm 89.20–37 Psalm 23	I Peter 3.8–18	or Ecclesiasticus 18.1–14
Proper 11		Ephesians 2.11–end		Hebrews 2.5–end
		Mark 6.30–34, 53–end		*HC* Luke 10.38–end
				or: 1st EP of Mary Magdalene:
				Psalm 139; Isaiah 25.1–9; 2 Corinthians 1.3–7
Monday	W	Song of Solomon 3.1–4	*MP* Psalms 30, 32, 150	*EP* Psalm 63
22 July		Psalm 42.1–10	I Samuel 16.14–end	Zephaniah 3.14–end
Mary Magdalene		2 Corinthians 5.14–17	Luke 8.1–3	Mark 15.40—16.7
		John 20.1–2, 11–18		
		Holy Communion	Morning Prayer	Evening Prayer
Tuesday	G	Micah 7.14–15, 18–20	Psalms 32, **36**	Psalm 33
23 July		Psalm 85.1–7	I Samuel 15.1–23	Ezekiel 33.1–20
Bridget, abbess, 1373		Matthew 12.46–end	Luke 23.26–43	James 2.14–end
DEL week 16				
Wednesday	G	Jeremiah 1.1, 4–10	Psalm 34	Psalm 119.33–56
24 July		Psalm 70	I Samuel 16	Ezekiel 33.21–end
		Matthew 13.1–9	Luke 23.44–56a	James 3
				or: 1st EP of James the Apostle:
				Psalm 144; Deuteronomy 30.11–end; Mark 5.21–end
		Principal Service	3rd Service	2nd Service
Thursday	R	Jeremiah 45.1–5 or Acts 11.27—12.2	*MP* Psalms 7, 29, 117	*EP* Psalm 94
25 July		Psalm 126	2 Kings 1.9–15	Jeremiah 26.1–15
James the Apostle		Acts 11.27—12.2 or 2 Corinthians 4.7–15	Luke 9.46–56	Mark 1.14–20
		Matthew 20.20–28		
		Holy Communion	Morning Prayer	Evening Prayer
Friday	Gw	Jeremiah 3.14–17	Psalm 31	Psalm 35
26 July		Psalm 23 or *Canticle:* Jeremiah 31.10–13	I Samuel 17.31–54	Ezekiel 34.17–end
Anne and Joachim, parents of the		Matthew 13.18–23	Luke 24.13–35	James 4.13—5.6
Blessed Virgin Mary		*Lesser Festival eucharistic lectionary:*		
		Zephaniah 3.14–18a; Psalm 127;		
		Romans 8.28–30; Matthew 13.16–17		
Saturday	G	Jeremiah 7.1–11	Psalms 41, **42, 43**	Psalms 45, **46**
27 July		Psalm 84.1–6	I Samuel 17.55—18.16	Ezekiel 36.16–36
Brooke Foss Westcott, bishop,		Matthew 13.24–30	Luke 24.36–end	James 5.7–end
teacher of the faith, 1901				

Trinity 9

		Principal Service		3rd Service	2nd Service
Sunday	**28 July** **9th Sunday after Trinity** Proper 12	G	*Continuous:* 2 Samuel 11.1–15 Psalm 14	*Related:* 2 Kings 4.42–end Psalm 145.10–19	Psalm 75 Song of Solomon 2 or 1 Maccabees 2.[1–14] 15–22	Psalm 74 [or 74.11–16] Job 19.1–27a or Ecclesiasticus 38.24–end
			Ephesians 3.14–end John 6.1–21		1 Peter 4.7–14	Hebrews 8 HC Luke 11.1–13
			Holy Communion	**Morning Prayer**	**Evening Prayer**
Monday	**29 July** Mary, Martha and Lazarus, companions of Our Lord DEL week 17	Gw	Jeremiah 13.1–11 Psalm 82 or Deuteronomy 32.18–21 Matthew 13.31–35		Psalm 44 1 Samuel 19.1–18 Acts 1.1–14	Psalm 47, 49 Ezekiel 37.1–14 Mark 1.1–13
			Lesser Festival eucharistic lectionary: Isaiah 25.6–9 Psalm 49.5–10, 16 Hebrews 2.10–15 John 12.1–8			
Tuesday	**30 July** William Wilberforce, social reformer, Olaudah Equiano and Thomas Clarkson anti-slavery campaigners, 1833, 1797 and 1846 (see p.83)	Gw	Jeremiah 14.17–end Psalm 79.8–end Matthew 13.36–43		Psalm 48, 52 1 Samuel 20.1–17 Acts 1.15–end	Psalm 50 Ezekiel 37.15–end Mark 1.14–20
Wednesday	**31 July** *Ignatius of Loyola, founder of the* *Society of Jesus, 1556*	G	Jeremiah 15.10, 16–end Psalm 59.1–4, 18–end Matthew 13.44–46		Psalm 119.57–80 (63*) 1 Samuel 20.18–end Acts 2.1–21	Psalm 59, 60 (67) Ezekiel 39.21–end Mark 1.21–28
Thursday	**1 August**	G	Jeremiah 18.1–6 Psalm 146.1–5 Matthew 13.47–53		Psalms 56, 57 (63*) 1 Samuel 21.1—22.5 Acts 2.22–36	Psalms 61, 62, 64 Ezekiel 43.1–12 Mark 1.29–end
Friday	**2 August**	G	Jeremiah 26.1–9 Psalm 69.4–10 Matthew 13.54–end		Psalms 51, 54 1 Samuel 22.6–end Acts 2.37–end	Psalm 38 Ezekiel 44.4–16 Mark 2.1–12
Saturday	**3 August**	G	Jeremiah 26.11–16, 24 Psalm 69.14–20 Matthew 14.1–12		Psalm 68 1 Samuel 23 Acts 3.1–10	Psalms 65, 66 Ezekiel 47.1–12 Mark 2.13–22

Trinity 10

	Principal Service	3rd Service	2nd Service
Sunday 4 August G **10th Sunday after Trinity** Proper 13	*Continuous:* 2 Samuel 11.26—12.13a Psalm 51.1-13 *Related:* Exodus 16.2-4, 9-15 Psalm 78.23-29 Ephesians 4.1-16 John 6.24-35	Psalm 86 Song of Solomon 5.2-end or 1 Maccabees 3.1-12 2 Peter 1.1-15	Psalm 88 [or 88.1-10] Job 28 or Ecclesiasticus 42.15-end Hebrews 11.17-31 HC Luke 12.13-21

	Holy Communion	Morning Prayer	Evening Prayer
Monday 5 August Gr Oswald, king, martyr, 642 (see p.79) DEL week 18	Jeremiah 28 Psalm 119.89-96 Matthew 14.13-21 or 14.22-end	Psalm 71 1 Samuel 24 Acts 3.11-end	Psalms 72, 75 Proverbs 1.1-19 Mark 2.23—3.6 *or:* 1st EP of the Transfiguration of Our Lord: Psalms 99, 110; Exodus 24.12-end; John 12.27-36a

	Principal Service	3rd Service	2nd Service
Tuesday 6 August Gold or W Transfiguration of Our Lord	Daniel 7.9-10, 13-14 Psalm 97 2 Peter 1.16-19 Luke 9.28-36	MP Psalms 27, 150 Ecclesiasticus 48.1-10 or 1 Kings 19.1-16 1 John 3.1-3	EP Psalm 72 Exodus 34.29-end 2 Corinthians 3

	Holy Communion	Morning Prayer	Evening Prayer
Wednesday 7 August G John Mason Neale, priest, hymn writer, 1866	Jeremiah 31.1-7 Psalm 121 Matthew 15.21-28	Psalm 77 1 Samuel 28.3-end Acts 4.13-31	Psalm 119.81-104 Proverbs 2 Mark 3.19b-end
Thursday 8 August Gw Dominic, priest, founder of the Order of Preachers, 1221 (see p.82)	Jeremiah 31.31-34 Psalm 51.11-18 Matthew 16.13-23	Psalm 78.1-39* 1 Samuel 31 Acts 4.32—5.11	Psalm 78.40-end* Proverbs 3.1-26 Mark 4.1-20
Friday 9 August Gw Mary Sumner, founder of the Mothers' Union, 1921 (see p.83)	Nahum 2.1, 3; 3.1-3, 6-7 Psalm 137.1-6 or Deuteronomy 32.35-36, 39, 41 Matthew 16.24-28	Psalm 55 2 Samuel 1 Acts 5.12-26	Psalm 69 Proverbs 3.27—4.19 Mark 4.21-34
Saturday 10 August Gr Laurence, deacon, martyr, 258 (see p.79)	Habakkuk 1.12—2.4 Psalm 9.7-11 Matthew 17.14-20	Psalms 76, 79 2 Samuel 2.1-11 Acts 5.27-end	Psalms 81, 84 Proverbs 6.1-19 Mark 4.35-end

Trinity 11

			Principal Service	3rd Service	2nd Service
Sunday	**11 August** **11th Sunday after Trinity** Proper 14	G	*Continuous:* 2 Samuel 18.5–9, 15, 31–33 Psalm 130 *Related:* 1 Kings 19.4–8 Psalm 34.1–8 Ephesians 4.25—5.2 John 6.35, 41–51	Psalm 90 Song of Solomon 8.5–7 or 1 Maccabees 14.4–15 2 Peter 3.8–13	Psalm 91 [or 91.1–12] Job 39.1—40.4 or Ecclesiasticus 43.13–end Hebrews 12.1–17 HC Luke 12.32–40
			Holy Communion	**Morning Prayer**	**Evening Prayer**
Monday	**12 August** DEL week 19	G	Ezekiel 1.2–5, 24–end Psalm 148.1–4, 12–13 Matthew 17.22–end	Psalms 80, 82 2 Samuel 3.12–end Acts 6	Psalms 85, 86 Proverbs 8.1–21 Mark 5.1–20
Tuesday	**13 August** Jeremy Taylor, bishop, teacher of the faith, 1667 (see p.80) Florence Nightingale, nurse, social reformer, 1910 Octavia Hill, social reformer, 1912	Gw	Ezekiel 2.8—3.4 Psalm 119.65–72 Matthew 18.1–5, 10, 12–14	Psalms 87, 89.1–18 2 Samuel 5.1–12 Acts 7.1–16	Psalm 89.19–end Proverbs 8.22–end Mark 5.21–34
Wednesday	**14 August** Maximilian Kolbe, friar, martyr, 1941	G	Ezekiel 9.1–7; 10.18–22 Psalm 113 Matthew 18.15–20	Psalm 119.105–128 2 Samuel 6.1–19 Acts 7.17–43	Psalms 91, 93 Proverbs 9 Mark 5.35–end or: 1st EP of the Blessed Virgin Mary: Psalm 72; Proverbs 8.22–31; John 19.23–27
			Principal Service	**3rd Service**	**2nd Service**
Thursday	**15 August** The Blessed Virgin Mary	W	Isaiah 61.10–end or Revelation 11.19—12.6, 10 Psalm 45.10–end Galatians 4.4–7 Luke 1.46–55	MP Psalms 98, 138, 147.1–12 Isaiah 7.10–15 Luke 11.27–28	EP Psalm 132 Song of Solomon 2.1–7 Acts 1.6–14
			Holy Communion	**Morning Prayer**	**Evening Prayer**
Friday	**16 August**	G	Ezekiel 16.1–15, 60–end Psalm 118.14–18 or Canticle: Song of Deliverance Matthew 19.3–12	Psalms 88 (95) 2 Samuel 7.18–end Acts 7.54—8.3	Psalm 102 Proverbs 11.1–12 Mark 6.14–29
Saturday	**17 August**	G	Ezekiel 18.1–11a, 13b, 30, 32 Psalm 51.1–3, 15–17 Matthew 19.13–15	Psalms 96, 97, 100 2 Samuel 9 Acts 8.4–25	Psalm 104 Proverbs 12.10–end Mark 6.30–44

Trinity 12

		Principal Service	3rd Service	2nd Service
Sunday	G			**Psalms [92] 100**
18 August **12th Sunday after Trinity** Proper 15		*Continuous:* 1 Kings 2.10–12; 3.3–14 Psalm 111 *Related:* Proverbs 9.1–6 Psalm 34.9–20 Ephesians 5.15–20 John 6.51–58	Psalm 106.1–10 Jonah 1 or Ecclesiasticus 3.1–15 2 Peter 3.14–end	Exodus 2.23—3.10 Hebrews 13.1–15 HC Luke 12.49–56
		Holy Communion	**Morning Prayer**	**Evening Prayer**
Monday **19 August** DEL week 20	G	Ezekiel 24.15–24 Psalm 78.1–8 Matthew 19.16–22	Psalms 98, 99, 101 2 Samuel 11 Acts 8.26–end	Psalm **105*** (or 103) Proverbs 14.31—15.17 Mark 6.45–end
Tuesday **20 August** Bernard, abbot, teacher of the faith, 1153 (see p.80) *William and Catherine Booth,* *founders of the Salvation Army, 1912, 1890*	Gw	Ezekiel 28.1–10 Psalm 107.1–3, 40, 43 Matthew 19.23–end	Psalm **106*** (or 103) 2 Samuel 12.1–25 Acts 9.1–19a	Psalm **107*** Proverbs 15.18–end Mark 7.1–13
Wednesday **21 August**	G	Ezekiel 34.1–11 Psalm 23 Matthew 20.1–16	Psalms 110, 111, 112 2 Samuel 15.1–12 Acts 9.19b–31	Psalm **119.129–152** Proverbs 18.10–end Mark 7.14–23
Thursday **22 August**	G	Ezekiel 36.23–28 Psalm 51.7–12 Matthew 22.1–14	Psalms **113, 115** 2 Samuel 15.13–end Acts 9.32–end	Psalms 114, **116**, 117 Proverbs 20.1–22 Mark 7.24–30
Friday **23 August**	G	Ezekiel 37.1–14 Psalm 107.1–8 Matthew 22.34–40	Psalm **139** 2 Samuel 16.1–14 Acts 10.1–16	Psalms **130**, 131, 137 Proverbs 22.1–16 Mark 7.31–end *or:* 1st EP of Bartholomew the Apostle: Psalm 97; Isaiah 61.1–9; 2 Corinthians 6.1–10
		Principal Service	**3rd Service**	**2nd Service**
Saturday **24 August** Bartholomew the Apostle	R	Isaiah 43.8–13 or Acts 5.12–16 Psalm 145.1–7 Acts 5.12–16 or 1 Corinthians 4.9–15 Luke 22.24–30	MP Psalms 86, 117 Genesis 28.10–17 John 1.43–end	EP Psalms 91, 116 Ecclesiasticus 39.1–10 or Deuteronomy 18.15–19 Matthew 10.1–22

Trinity 13

		Principal Service		3rd Service	2nd Service
		Holy Communion		**Morning Prayer**	**Evening Prayer**
Sunday	**25 August** **13th Sunday after Trinity** Proper 16 G	*Continuous* 1 Kings 8.[1, 6, 10–11] 22–30, 41–43 Psalm 84	*Related:* Joshua 24.1–2a, 14–18 Psalm 34.15–end Ephesians 6.10–20 John 6.56–69	Psalm 115 Jonah 2 or Ecclesiasticus 3.17–29 Revelation 1	Psalm 116 [or 116.10–end] Exodus 4.27—5.1 Hebrews 13.16–21 HC Luke 13.10–17
Monday	**26 August** DEL week 21 G	2 Thessalonians 1.1–5, 11–end Psalm 39.1–9 Matthew 23.13–22		Psalms 123, 124, 125, **126** 2 Samuel 18.1–18 Acts 10.34–end	Psalms **127**, 128, 129 Proverbs 25.1–14 Mark 8.11–21
Tuesday	**27 August** Monica, mother of Augustine of Hippo, 387 (see p.83) Gw	2 Thessalonians 2.1–3a, 14–end Psalm 98 Matthew 23.23–26		Psalms **132**, 133 2 Samuel 18.19–19.8a Acts 11.1–18	Psalms (134), **135** Proverbs 25.15–end Mark 8.22–26
Wednesday	**28 August** Augustine, bishop, teacher of the faith, 430 (see p.80) Gw	2 Thessalonians 3.6–10, 16–end Psalm 128 Matthew 23.27–32		Psalm **119.153–end** 2 Samuel 19.8b–23 Acts 11.19–end	Psalm **136** Proverbs 26.12–end Mark 8.27–9.1
Thursday	**29 August** Beheading of John the Baptist Gr	1 Corinthians 1.1–9 Psalm 145.1–7 Matthew 24.42–end *Lesser Festival eucharistic lectionary:* Jeremiah 1.4–10 Psalm 11 Hebrews 11.32—12.2 Matthew 14.1–12		Psalms **143**, 146 2 Samuel 19.24–end Acts 12.1–17	Psalms **138**, 140, 141 Proverbs 27.1–22 Mark 9.2–13
Friday	**30 August** John Bunyan, spiritual writer, 1688 (see p.80) Gw	1 Corinthians 1.17–25 Psalm 33.6–12 Matthew 25.1–13		Psalms **142**, **144** 2 Samuel 23.1–7 Acts 12.18–end	Psalm **145** Proverbs 30.1–9, 24–31 Mark 9.14–29
Saturday	**31 August** Aidan, bishop, missionary, 651 (see p.82) Gw	1 Corinthians 1.26–end Psalm 33.12–15, 20–end Matthew 25.14–30		Psalm **147** 2 Samuel 24 Acts 13.1–12	Psalms **148**, 149, 150 Proverbs 31.10–end Mark 9.30–37

Trinity 14

	Principal Service	3rd Service	2nd Service
Sunday 1 September **14th Sunday after Trinity** Proper 17 G	*Continuous:* Song of Solomon 2.8–13 Psalm 45.1–2, 6–9 [or 45.1–7] *Related:* Deuteronomy 4.1–2, 6–9 Psalm 15 James 1.17–end Mark 7.1–8, 14–15, 21–23	Psalm 119.17–40 Jonah 3.1–9 or Ecclesiasticus 11.7–28 (or 19–28) Revelation 3.14–end	Psalm 119.1–16 [or 119.9–16] Exodus 12.21–27 Matthew 4.23–5.20
	Holy Communion	**Morning Prayer**	**Evening Prayer**
Monday 2 September *Martyrs of Papua New Guinea, 1901, 1942* DEL week 22 G	1 Corinthians 2.1–5 Psalm 33.12–21 Luke 4.16–30	Psalms 1, 2, 3 1 Kings 1.5–31 Acts 13.13–43	Psalms **4**, **7** Wisdom 1 or 1 Chronicles 10.1—11.9 Mark 9.38–end
Tuesday 3 September *Gregory the Great, bishop, teacher of the faith, 604* (see p.80) Gw	1 Corinthians 2.10b–end Psalm 145.10–17 Luke 4.31–37	Psalms **5**, 6 (8) 1 Kings 1.32—2.4; 2.10–12 Acts 13.44—14.7	Psalms **9**, 10* Wisdom 2 or 1 Chronicles 13 Mark 10.1–16
Wednesday 4 September *Birinus, bishop, 650* G	1 Corinthians 3.1–9 Psalm 62 Luke 4.38–end	Psalm 119.1–32 1 Kings 3 Acts 14.8–end	Psalms 11, **12**, 13 Wisdom 3.1–9 or 1 Chronicles 15.1—16.3 Mark 10.17–31
Thursday 5 September G	1 Corinthians 3.18–end Psalm 24.1–6 Luke 5.1–11	Psalms 14, **15**, 16 1 Kings 4.29—5.12 Acts 15.1–21	Psalm 18* Wisdom 4.7–end or 1 Chronicles 17 Mark 10.32–34
Friday 6 September *Allen Gardiner, missionary, founder of the South American Mission Society, 1851* G	1 Corinthians 4.1–5 Psalm 37.3–8 Luke 5.33–end	Psalms 17, **19** 1 Kings 6.1, 11–28 Acts 15.22–35	Psalm 22 Wisdom 5.1–16 or 1 Chronicles 21.1—22.1 Mark 10.35–45
Saturday 7 September G	1 Corinthians 4.6–15 Psalm 145.18–end Luke 6.1–5	Psalms 21, **23** 1 Kings 8.1–30 Acts 15.36—16.5	Psalms **24**, 25 Wisdom 5.17—6.11 or 1 Chronicles 22.2–end Mark 10.46–end

or, if the Blessed Virgin Mary is transferred to 8 September, the provision for the 1st EP (14 August) may be used.

		Principal Service	2nd Service	3rd Service
Sunday	**8 September** **15th Sunday after Trinity** Proper 18 Accession of King Charles III, 2022 (see p.85) G	*Continuous:* Proverbs 22.1–2, 8, 9, 22, 23 Psalm 125 James 2.1–10 [11–13] 14–17 Mark 7.24–end *Related:* Isaiah 35.4–7a Psalm 146	Psalm 119.41–56 [or 119.49–56] Exodus 14.5–end Matthew 6.1–18	Psalm 119.57–72 Jonah 3.10—4.11 *or* Ecclesiasticus 27.30—28.9 Revelation 8.1–5

If the Blessed Virgin Mary is transferred to 8 September, the provision (including 1st EP) for 15 August is used.

		Holy Communion	Morning Prayer	Evening Prayer
Monday	**9 September** *Charles Fuge Lowder, priest, 1880* DEL week 23 G	1 Corinthians 5.1–8 Psalm 5.5–9a Luke 6.6–11	Psalms 27, 30 1 Kings 8.31–62 Acts 16.6–24	Psalms 26, **28**, 29 Wisdom 6.12–23 *or* 1 Chronicles 28. 1–10 Mark 11.1–11
Tuesday	**10 September** G	1 Corinthians 6.1–11 Psalm 149.1–5 Luke 6.12–19	Psalms 32, **36** 1 Kings 8.63—9.9 Acts 16.25–end	Psalm **33** Wisdom 7.1–14 *or* 1 Chronicles 28.11–end Mark 11.12–26
Wednesday	**11 September** G	1 Corinthians 7.25–31 Psalm 45.11–end Luke 6.20–26	Psalm **34** 1 Kings 10.1–25 Acts 17.1–15	Psalm **119.33–56** Wisdom 7.15—8.4 *or* 1 Chronicles 29.1–9 Mark 11.27–end
Thursday	**12 September** G	1 Corinthians 8.1–7, 11–end Psalm 139.1–9 Luke 6.27–38	Psalm **37*** 1 Kings 11.1–13 Acts 17.16–end	Psalms 39, **40** Wisdom 8.5–18 *or* 1 Chronicles 29.10–20 Mark 12.1–12
Friday	**13 September** *John Chrysostom, bishop,* *teacher of the faith, 407 (see p.80)* Gw	1 Corinthians 9.16–19, 22–end Psalm 84.1–6 Luke 6.39–42	Psalm **31** 1 Kings 11.26–end Acts 18.1–21	Psalm **35** Wisdom 8.21—end of 9 *or* 1 Chronicles 29.21–end Mark 12.13–17 *or:* 1st EP of Holy Cross Day: Psalm 66; Isaiah 52.13—end of 53; Ephesians 2.11–end

		Principal Service	3rd Service	2nd Service
Saturday	**14 September** Holy Cross Day R	Numbers 21.4–9 Psalm 22.23–28 Philippians 2.6–11 John 3.13–17	MP Psalms 2, 8, 146 Genesis 3.1–15 John 12.27–36a	EP Psalms 110, 150 Isaiah 63.1–16 1 Corinthians 1.18–25

Trinity 16

	Date / Commemoration	Principal Service / Holy Communion	3rd Service / Morning Prayer	2nd Service / Evening Prayer
Sunday	**15 September** G **16th Sunday after Trinity** Proper 19	*Continuous:* Proverbs 1.20-33 Psalm 19 [or 19.1-6] *or Canticle:* Wisdom 7.26—8.1 *Related:* Isaiah 50.4-9a Psalm 116.1-8 James 3.1-12 Mark 8.27-end	Psalm 119.105-120 Isaiah 44.24—45.8 Revelation 12.1-12	Psalm 119.73-88 [or 119.73-80] Exodus 18.13-26 Matthew 7.1-14
		Holy Communion	**Morning Prayer**	**Evening Prayer**
Monday	**16 September** Gw Ninian, bishop, apostle of the Picts, c.432 (see p.82) *Edward Bouverie Pusey, priest, 1882* DEL week 24	1 Corinthians 11.17-26, 33 Psalm 40.7-11 Luke 7.1-10	Psalm 44 1 Kings 12.25—13.10 Acts 19.8-20	Psalms 47, 49 Wisdom 11.21—12.2 or 2 Chronicles 2.1-16 Mark 12.28-34
Tuesday	**17 September** Gw Hildegard, abbess, visionary, 1179 (see p.82)	1 Corinthians 12.12-14, 27-end Psalm 100 Luke 7.11-17	Psalms 48, 52 1 Kings 13.11-end Acts 19.21-end	Psalm 50 Wisdom 12.12-21 or 2 Chronicles 3 Mark 12.35-end
Wednesday	**18 September** G	1 Corinthians 12.31b—end of 13 Psalm 33.1-12 Luke 7.31-35	Psalm 119.57-80 1 Kings 17 Acts 20.1-16	Psalms 59, 60 (67) Wisdom 13.1-9 or 2 Chronicles 5 Mark 13.1-13
Thursday	**19 September** G *Theodore, archbishop, 690*	1 Corinthians 15.1-11 Psalm 118.1-2, 17-20 Luke 7.36-end	Psalms 56, 57 (63*) 1 Kings 18.1-20 Acts 20.17-end	Psalms 61, 62, 64 Wisdom 16.15—17.1 or 2 Chronicles 6.1-21 Mark 13.14-23
Friday	**20 September** Gr John Coleridge Patteson, bishop, and companions, martyrs, 1871 (see p.79)	1 Corinthians 15.12-20 Psalm 17.1-8 Luke 8.1-3	Psalms 51, 54 1 Kings 18.21-end Acts 21.1-16	Psalm 38 Wisdom 18.6-19 or 2 Chronicles 6.22-end Mark 13.24-31 *or:* 1st EP of Matthew, Apostle and Evangelist: Psalm 34; Isaiah 33.13-17; Matthew 6.19-end
		Principal Service	**3rd Service**	**2nd Service**
Saturday	**21 September** R Matthew, Apostle and Evangelist	Proverbs 3.13-18 Psalm 119.65-72 2 Corinthians 4.1-6 Matthew 9.9-13	MP Psalms 49, 117 1 Kings 19.15-end 2 Timothy 3.14-end	EP Psalm 119.33-40, 89-96 Ecclesiastes 5.4-12 Matthew 19.16-end

Trinity 17

	Principal Service	3rd Service	2nd Service
Sunday **22 September** G **17th Sunday after Trinity** Proper 20	Continuous: Proverbs 31.10–end Psalm 1 / Related: Wisdom 1.16—2.1, 12–22 or Jeremiah 11.18–20 Psalm 54 / James 3.13—4.3, 7–8a / Mark 9.30–37	Psalm 119.153–end Isaiah 45.9–22 Revelation 14.1–5	Psalm 119.137–152 [or 119.137–144] Exodus 19.10–end Matthew 8.23–end

	Holy Communion	Morning Prayer	Evening Prayer
Monday **23 September** G DEL week 25	Proverbs 3.27–34 Psalm 15 Luke 8.16–18	Psalm 71 1 Kings 21 Acts 21.37—22.21	Psalms 72, 75 1 Maccabees 1.1–19 or 2 Chronicles 9.1–12 Mark 14.1–11
Tuesday **24 September** G	Proverbs 21.1–6, 10–13 Psalm 119.1–8 Luke 8.19–21	Psalm 73 1 Kings 22.1–28 Acts 22.22—23.11	Psalm 74 1 Maccabees 1.20–40 or 2 Chronicles 10.1—11.4 Mark 14.12–25
Wednesday **25 September** Gw Lancelot Andrewes, bishop, spiritual writer, 1626 (see p.81) *Sergei of Radonezh, monastic reformer, teacher of the faith, 1392* Ember Day	Proverbs 30.5–9 Psalm 119.105–112 Luke 9.1–6	Psalm 77 1 Kings 22.29–45 Acts 23.12–end	Psalm 119.81–104 1 Maccabees 1.41–end or 2 Chronicles 12 Mark 14.26–42
Thursday **26 September** G Wilson Carlile, *founder of the Church Army, 1942*	Ecclesiastes 1.2–11 Psalm 90.1–6 Luke 9.7–9	Psalm 78.1–39* 2 Kings 1.2–17 Acts 24.1–23	Psalm 78.40–end* 1 Maccabees 2.1–28 or 2 Chronicles 13.1—14.1 Mark 14.43–52
Friday **27 September** Gw Vincent de Paul, *founder of the Lazarists, 1660 (see p.82)* Ember Day	Ecclesiastes 3.1–11 Psalm 144.1–4 Luke 9.18–22	Psalm 55 2 Kings 2.1–18 Acts 24.24—25.12	Psalm 69 1 Maccabees 2.29–48 or 2 Chronicles 14.2–end Mark 14.53–65
Saturday **28 September** G Ember Day	Ecclesiastes 11.9—12.8 Psalm 90.1–2, 12–end Luke 9.43b–45	Psalms 76, 79 2 Kings 4.1–37 Acts 25.13–end	Psalms 81, 84 1 Maccabees 2.49–end or 2 Chronicles 15.1–15 Mark 14.66–end

or, if Michael and All Angels is celebrated on Sunday 29 September,
1st EP of Michael and All Angels:
Psalm 91; 2 Kings 6.8–17; Matthew 18.1–6, 10

Michael and All Angels / Trinity 18

If Michael and All Angels is celebrated on Sunday 29 September:

		Principal Service	3rd Service	2nd Service
Sunday	**29 September** W Michael and All Angels	Genesis 28.10–17 or Revelation 12.7–12 Psalm 103.19–end Revelation 12.7–12 or Hebrews 1.5–end John 1.47–end	MP Psalms 34, 150 Tobit 12.6–end or Daniel 12.1–4 Acts 12.1–11	EP Psalms 138, 148 Daniel 10.4–end Revelation 5

		Holy Communion	Morning Prayer	Evening Prayer
Monday	**30 September** G *Jerome, translator, teacher of the faith, 420* DEL week 26	Job 1.6–end Psalm 17.1–11 Luke 9.46–50	Psalms 80, 82 2 Kings 5 Acts 26.1–23	Psalms 85, 86 1 Maccabees 3.1–26 or 2 Chronicles 17.1–12 Mark 15.1–15

If Michael and All Angels is transferred to Monday 30 September:

		Principal Service	3rd Service	2nd Service
Sunday	**29 September** G **18th Sunday after Trinity** Proper 21	*Continuous:* Esther 7.1–6, 9–10; 9. 20–22 Psalm 124 *Related:* Numbers 11.4–6, 10–16, 24–29 Psalm 19.7–end James 5.13–end Mark 9.38–end	Psalm 122 Isaiah 48.12–end Luke 11.37–end	Psalms 120, 121 Exodus 24 Matthew 9.1–8 or: 1st EP of Michael and All Angels: Psalm 91; 2 Kings 6.8–17; Matthew 18.1–6,10
Monday	**30 September** W Michael and All Angels *(transferred from 29 September)*	Genesis 28.10–17 or Revelation 12.7–12 Psalm 103.19–end Revelation 12.7–12 or Hebrews 1.5–end John 1.47–end	MP Psalms 34, 150 Tobit 12.6–end or Daniel 12.1–4 Acts 12.1–11	EP Psalms 138, 148 Daniel 10.4–end Revelation 5

		Holy Communion	Morning Prayer	Evening Prayer
Tuesday 1 October *Remigius, bishop, 533* *Anthony Ashley Cooper (Earl of Shaftesbury),* *social reformer, 1885* DEL week 26	G	Job 3.1–3, 11–17, 20–23 Psalm 88.14–19 Luke 9.51–56	Psalms 87, **89**.1–18 2 Kings 6.1–23 Acts 26.24–end	Psalm **89**.19–end 1 Maccabees 3.27–41 or 2 Chronicles 18.1–27 Mark 15.16–32
Wednesday 2 October	G	Job 9.1–12, 14–16 Psalm 88.1–6, 11 Luke 9.57–end	Psalm 119.**105–128** 2 Kings 9.1–16 Acts 27.1–26	Psalms **91**, **93** 1 Maccabees 3.42–end or 2 Chronicles 18.28—end of 19 Mark 15.33–41
Thursday 3 October *George Bell, bishop, ecumenist, peacemaker,* *1958*	G	Job 19.21–27a Psalm 27.13–16 Luke 10.1–12	Psalms 90, **92** 2 Kings 9.17–end Acts 27.27–end	Psalm **94** 1 Maccabees 4.1–25 or 2 Chronicles 20.1–23 Mark 15.42–end
Friday 4 October *Francis of Assisi, friar, deacon, 1226* *(see p.82)*	Gw	Job 38.1, 12–21; 40.3–5 Psalm 139.1–6, 11 Luke 10.13–16	Psalms **88** (**95**) 2 Kings 12.1–19 Acts 28.1–16	Psalm **102** 1 Maccabees 4.26–35 or 2 Chronicles 22.10—end of 23 Mark 16.1–8
Saturday 5 October	G	Job 42.1–3, 6, 12–end Psalm 119.169–end Luke 10.17–24	Psalms 96, **97**, **100** 2 Kings 17.1–23 Acts 28.17–end	Psalm **104** 1 Maccabees 4.36–end or 2 Chronicles 24.1–22 Mark 16.9–end

Trinity 19

	Principal Service		3rd Service	2nd Service
	Holy Communion		Morning Prayer	Evening Prayer
Sunday **6 October** G **19th Sunday after Trinity** Proper 22	*Continuous:* Job 1.1; 2.1–10 Psalm 26	*Related:* Genesis 2.18–24 Psalm 8 Hebrews 1.1–4; 2.5–12 Mark 10.2–16	Psalms 123, 124 Isaiah 49.13–23 Luke 12.1–12	Psalms 125, 126 Joshua 3.7–end Matthew 10.1–22
Monday **7 October** G DEL week 27	Galatians 1.6–12 Psalm 111.1–6 Luke 10.25–37		Psalms 98, 99, 101 2 Kings 17.24–end Philippians 1.1–11	Psalm 105* (or 103) 1 Maccabees 6.1–17 or 2 Chronicles 26.1–21 John 13.1–11
Tuesday **8 October** G	Galatians 1.13–end Psalm 139.1–9 Luke 10.38–end		Psalm 106* (or 103) 2 Kings 18.1–12 Philippians 1.12–end	Psalm 107* 1 Maccabees 6.18–47 or 2 Chronicles 28 John 13.12–20
Wednesday **9 October** G *Denys, bishop, and companions, martyrs, c.250* *Robert Grosseteste, bishop, philosopher, scientist, 1253*	Galatians 2.1–2,7–14 Psalm 117 Luke 11.1–4		Psalms 110, 111, 112 2 Kings 18.13–end Philippians 2.1–13	Psalm 119.129–152 1 Maccabees 7.1–20 or 2 Chronicles 29.1–19 John 13.21–30
Thursday **10 October** Gw *Paulinus, bishop, missionary, 644* *(see p.82)* *Thomas Traherne, poet, spiritual writer, 1674*	Galatians 3.1–5 *Canticle: Benedictus* Luke 11.5–13		Psalms 113, 115 2 Kings 19.1–19 Philippians 2.14–end	Psalms 114, 116, 117 1 Maccabees 7.21–end or 2 Chronicles 29.20–end John 13.31–end
Friday **11 October** G *Ethelburga, abbess, 675* *James the Deacon, companion of Paulinus, 7th cent.*	Galatians 3.7–14 Psalm 111.4–end Luke 11.15–26		Psalm 139 2 Kings 19.20–36 Philippians 3.1—4.1	Psalms 130, 131, 137 1 Maccabees 9.1–22 or 2 Chronicles 30 John 14.1–14
Saturday **12 October** Gw *Wilfrid, bishop, missionary, 709* *(see p.82)* *Elizabeth Fry, prison reformer, 1845* *Edith Cavell, nurse, 1915*	Galatians 3.22–end Psalm 105.1–7 Luke 11.27–28		Psalms 120, 121, 122 2 Kings 20 Philippians 4.2–end	Psalm 118 1 Maccabees 13.41–end, 14.4–15 or 2 Chronicles 32.1–22 John 14.15–end

Trinity 20

		Principal Service		3rd Service	2nd Service
Sunday	G	*Continuous:*	*Related:*	Psalms 129, 130	Psalms 127 [128]
13 October		Job 23.1–9, 16–end	Amos 5.6–7, 10–15	Isaiah 50.4–10	Joshua 5.13—6.20
20th Sunday after Trinity		Psalm 22.1–15	Psalm 90.12–end	Luke 13.22–30	Matthew 11.20–end
Proper 23			Hebrews 4.12–end		
			Mark 10.17–31		

		Holy Communion	Morning Prayer	Evening Prayer
Monday	G	Galatians 4.21–24, 26–27, 31, 5.1	Psalms 123, 124, 125, **126**	Psalms **127**, 128, 129
14 October		Psalm 113	2 Kings 21.1–18	2 Maccabees 4.7–17
DEL week 28		Luke 11.29–32	1 Timothy 1.1–17	or 2 Chronicles 33.1–13
				John 15.1–11
Tuesday	Gw	Galatians 5.1–6	Psalms **132**, 133	Psalms (134), **135**
15 October		Psalm 119.41–48	2 Kings 22.1–23.3	2 Maccabees 6.12–end
Teresa of Avila, teacher of the faith, 1582		Luke 11.37–41	1 Timothy 1.18—end of 2	or 2 Chronicles 34.1–18
(see p.80)				John 15.12–17
Wednesday	G	Galatians 5.18–end	Psalm **119.153–end**	Psalm **136**
16 October		Psalm 1	2 Kings 23.4–25	2 Maccabees 7.1–19
Nicholas Ridley and Hugh Latimer, bishops, martyrs, 1555		Luke 11.42–46	1 Timothy 3	or 2 Chronicles 34.19–end
				John 15.18–end
Thursday	Gr	Ephesians 1.1–10	Psalms **143**, 146	Psalms **138**, 140, 141
17 October		Psalm 98.1–4	2 Kings 23.36—24.17	2 Maccabees 7.20–41
Ignatius, bishop, martyr, c.107 (see p.79)		Luke 11.47–end	1 Timothy 4	or 2 Chronicles 35.1–19
				John 16.1–15
				or: 1st EP of Luke the Evangelist:
				Psalm 33; Hosea 6.1–3; 2 Timothy 3.10–end

		Principal Service	3rd Service	2nd Service
Friday	R	Isaiah 35.3–6 or Acts 16.6–12a	MP Psalms 145, 146	EP Psalms 103
18 October		Psalm 147.1–7	Isaiah 55	Ecclesiasticus 38.1–14
Luke the Evangelist		2 Timothy 4.5–17	Luke 1.1–4	or Isaiah 61.1–6
		Luke 10.1–9		Colossians 4.7–end

		Holy Communion	Morning Prayer	Evening Prayer
Saturday	Gw	Ephesians 1.15–end	Psalm **147**	Psalms **148**, 149, 150
19 October		Psalm 8	2 Kings 25.22–end	Tobit 2
Henry Martyn, translator, missionary, 1812 (see p.82)		Luke 12.8–12	1 Timothy 5.17–end	or 2 Chronicles 36.11–end
				John 16.23–end

		Principal Service		3rd Service	2nd Service
Sunday	**20 October** G **21st Sunday after Trinity** Proper 24	*Continuous:* Job 38.1–7 [34–end] Psalm 104.1–10, 26, 35c [or 104.1–10]	*Related:* Isaiah 53.4–end Psalm 91.9–end Hebrews 5.1–10 Mark 10.35–45	Psalms 133, 134, 137.1–6 Isaiah 54.1–14 Luke 13.31–end	Psalm 141 Joshua 14.6–14 Matthew 12.1–21
		Holy Communion		**Morning Prayer**	**Evening Prayer**
Monday	**21 October** G DEL week 29	Ephesians 2.1–10 Psalm 100 Luke 12.13–21		Psalms 1, 2, 3 Judith 4 or Exodus 22.21–27; 23.1–17 1 Timothy 6.1–10	Psalms 4, 7 Tobit 3 or Micah 1.1–9 John 17.1–5
Tuesday	**22 October** G	Ephesians 2.12–end Psalm 85.7–end Luke 12.35–38		Psalms 5, 6 (8) Judith 5.1–6.4 or Exodus 29.38—30.16 1 Timothy 6.11–end	Psalms 9, 10* Tobit 4 or Micah 2 John 17.6–19
Wednesday	**23 October** G	Ephesians 3.2–12 Psalm 98 Luke 12.39–48		Psalm 119.1–32 Judith 6.10—7.7 or Leviticus 8 2 Timothy 1.1–14	Psalms 11, 12, 13 Tobit 5.1–6.1a or Micah 3 John 17.20–end
Thursday	**24 October** G	Ephesians 3.14–end Psalm 33.1–6 Luke 12.49–53		Psalms 14, 15, 16 Judith 7.19–end or Leviticus 9 2 Timothy 1.15—2.13	Psalm 18* Tobit 6.1b–end or Micah 4.1—5.1 John 18.1–11
Friday	**25 October** G *Crispin and Crispinian, martyrs, c.287*	Ephesians 4.1–6 Psalm 24.1–6 Luke 12.54–end		Psalms 17, 19 Judith 8.9–end or Leviticus 16.2–24 2 Timothy 2.14–end	Psalm 22 Tobit 7 or Micah 5.2–end John 18.12–27
Saturday	**26 October** Gw *Alfred, king, scholar, 899 (see p.83) Cedd, abbot, bishop, 664*	Ephesians 4.7–16 Psalm 122 Luke 13.1–9		Psalms 20, 21, 23 Judith 9 or Leviticus 17 2 Timothy 3	Psalms 24, 25 Tobit 8 or Micah 6 John 18.28–end

Last after Trinity

		Principal Service	3rd Service	2nd Service
Sunday	**27 October** G **Last Sunday after Trinity** Proper 25	*Continuous:* Job 42.1–6, 10–end Psalm 34.1–8, 19–end [or 34.1–8] *Related:* Jeremiah 31.7–9 Psalm 126 Hebrews 7.23–end Mark 10.46–end	Psalm 119.89–104 Isaiah 59.9–20 Luke 14.1–14	Psalm 119.121–136 Ecclesiastes 11, 12 2 Timothy 2.1–7 HC Luke 18.9–14 *or:* 1st EP of Simon and Jude, Apostles:
				Psalms 124, 125, 126; Deuteronomy 32.1–4; John 14.15–26
or Sunday	**27 October** G Bible Sunday	Isaiah 55.1–11 Psalm 19.7–end 2 Timothy 3.14—4.5 John 5.36b–end	Psalm 119.89–104 Isaiah 45.22–end Matthew 24.30–35 or Luke 14.1–14	Psalm 119.1–16 2 Kings 22 Colossians 3.12–17 HC Luke 4.14–30 *or:* 1st EP of Simon and Jude, Apostles:
				Psalms 124, 125, 126; Deuteronomy 32.1–4; John 14.15–26

or, if the date of dedication of a church is not known, the Dedication Festival (Gold or W) may be celebrated today or on 6 October, or on a suitable date chosen locally (see p.78).

Monday	**28 October** R Simon and Jude, Apostles	Isaiah 28.14–16 Psalm 119.89–96 Ephesians 2.19–end John 15.17–end	MP Psalms 116, 117 Wisdom 5.1–16 or Isaiah 45.18–end Luke 6.12–16	EP Psalm 119.1–16 1 Maccabees 2.42–66 or Jeremiah 3.11–18 Jude 1–4, 17–end

		Holy Communion	Morning Prayer	Evening Prayer
Tuesday	**29 October** Gr James Hannington, bishop, martyr, 1885 (see p.79) DEL week 30	Ephesians 5.21–end Psalm 128 Luke 13.18–21	Psalms 32, 36 Judith 11 or Leviticus 23.1–22 2 Timothy 4.9–end	Psalm 33 Tobit 10 or Micah 7.8–end John 19.17–30
Wednesday	**30 October** G	Ephesians 6.1–9 Psalm 145.10–20 Luke 13.22–30	Psalm 34 Judith 12 or Leviticus 23.23–end Titus 1	Psalm 119.33–56 Tobit 11 or Habakkuk 1.1–11 John 19.31–end
Thursday	**31 October** G *Martin Luther, reformer, 1546*	Ephesians 6.10–20 Psalm 144.1–2, 9–11 Luke 13.31–end	Psalm 37* Judith 13 or Leviticus 24.1–9 Titus 2	Psalms 39, 40 Tobit 12 or Habakkuk 1.12—2.5 John 20.1–10 *or, if All Saints' Day is celebrated on Friday 1 November only:* **1st EP of All Saints' Day:** Psalms 1, 5; Ecclesiasticus 44.1–15 or Isaiah 40.27–end; Revelation 19.6–10

All Saints' Day / 4 before Advent

All Saints' Day is celebrated on Friday 1 November or on Sunday 3 November; if the latter there may be a supplementary celebration on 1 November.
If All Saints' Day is celebrated on Friday 1 November:

		Principal Service	3rd Service	2nd Service
Friday **1 November** All Saints' Day	*Gold or W*	Wisdom 3.1–9 or Isaiah 25.6–9 Psalm 24.1–6 Revelation 21.1–6a John 11.32–44	MP Psalms 15, 84, 149 Isaiah 35.1–9 Luke 9.18–27	EP Psalms 148, 150 Isaiah 65.17–end Hebrews 11.32—12.2

If All Saints' Day is celebrated on Friday 1 November in addition to Sunday 3 November:

		Principal Service	3rd Service	2nd Service
Friday **1 November** All Saints' Day	*Gold or W*	Isaiah 56.3–8 or 2 Esdras 2.42–end Psalm 33.1–5 Hebrews 12.18–24 Matthew 5.1–12	MP Psalm 111, 112, 117 Wisdom 5.1–16 or Jeremiah 31.31–34 2 Corinthians 4.5–12	EP Psalm 145 Isaiah 66.20–23 Colossians 1.9–14

		Holy Communion	Morning Prayer	Evening Prayer
Saturday **2 November** Commemoration of the Faithful Departed (All Souls' Day)	*Rp/Gp*	Philippians 1.18–26 Psalm 42.1–7 Luke 14.1, 7–11 *Lesser Festival eucharistic lectionary:* Lamentations 3.17–26, 31–33 or Wisdom 3.1–9 Psalm 23 or 27.1–6,16–end Romans 5.5–11 or 1 Peter 1.3–9 John 5.19–25 or John 6.37–40	Psalms 41, **42**, 43 Judith 15.14–end of 16 or Numbers 6.1–5, 21–end Philemon	Psalms **45**, **46** Tobit 14.2–end or Habakkuk 3.2–19a John 20.19–end

		Principal Service	3rd Service	2nd Service
Sunday **3 November** **4th Sunday before Advent**	*R/G*	Deuteronomy 6.1–9 Psalm 119.1–8 Hebrews 9.11–14 Mark 12.28–34	Psalms 112, 149 Jeremiah 31.31–34 1 John 3.1–3	Psalm 145 [or 145.1–9] Daniel 2.1–48 (or 1–11, 25–48) Revelation 7.9–end HC Matthew 5.1–12

All Saints' Day / 4 before Advent

If All Saints' Day is celebrated on Sunday 3 November only:

		Holy Communion	Morning Prayer	Evening Prayer
Friday	**1 November**	G	Philippians 1.1–11 Psalm 111 Luke 14.1–6	Psalm **31** Judith 15.1–13 or Leviticus 25.1–24 Titus 3	Psalm **35** Tobit 13.1—14.1 or Habakkuk 2.6–end John 20.11–18
Saturday	**2 November** Commemoration of the Faithful Departed (All Souls' Day)	Gp	Philippians 1.18–26 Psalm 42.1–7 Luke 14.1, 7–11 *Lesser Festival eucharistic lectionary:* Lamentations 3.17–26, 31–33 or Wisdom 3.1–9 Psalm 23 or 27.1–6, 16–end Romans 5.5–11 or 1 Peter 1.3–9 John 5.19–25 or John 6.37–40	Psalms 41, **42**, 43 Judith 15.14—end of 16 or Numbers 6.1–5, 21–end Philemon	Psalms 45, **46** Tobit 14.2–end or Habakkuk 3.2–19a John 20.19–end
					1st EP of All Saints' Day: Psalms 1, 5; Ecclesiasticus 44.1–15 or Isaiah 40.27–end; Revelation 19.6–10

		Principal Service	3rd Service	2nd Service
Sunday	**3 November** All Saints' Day	*Gold or* W	Wisdom 3.1–9 or Isaiah 25.6–9 Psalm 24.1–6 Revelation 21.1–6a John 11.32–44	*MP* Psalms 15, 84, 149 Isaiah 35.1–9 Luke 9.18–27	*EP* Psalms 148, 150 Isaiah 65.17–end Hebrews 11.32—12.2

		Holy Communion	Morning Prayer	Evening Prayer
Monday	**4 November** R/G DEL week 31	Philippians 2.1–4 Psalm 131 Luke 14.12–14	Psalms **2**, 146 or **44** Daniel 1 Revelation 1	Psalm **92**, 96, 97 or **47**, 49 Isaiah 1.1–20 Matthew 1.18–end
Tuesday	**5 November** R/G	Philippians 2.5–11 Psalm 22.22–27 Luke 14.15–24	Psalms **5**, 147.1–12 or **48**, 52 Daniel 2.1–24 Revelation 2.1–11	Psalms 98, 99, **100** or **50** Isaiah 1.21–end Matthew 2.1–15
Wednesday	**6 November** R/G *Leonard, hermit, 6th cent.* *William Temple, archbishop,* *teacher of the faith, 1944*	Philippians 2.12–18 Psalm 27.1–5 Luke 14.25–33	Psalms **9**, 147.13–end or **119.57–80** Daniel 2.25–end Revelation 2.12–end	Psalm 111, **112**, 116 or **59**, 60 (67) Isaiah 2.1–11 Matthew 2.16–end
Thursday	**7 November** Rw/Gw Willibrord, bishop, 739 (see p.82)	Philippians 3.3–8a Psalm 105.1–7 Luke 15.1–10	Psalms 11, **15**, 148 or 56, **57** (63*) Daniel 3.1–18 Revelation 3.1–13	Psalm 118 or 61, **62**, 64 Isaiah 2.12–end Matthew 3
Friday	**8 November** Rw/Gw Saints and Martyrs of England	Philippians 3.17—4.1 Psalm 122 Luke 16.1–8 *Lesser Festival eucharistic lectionary:* Isaiah 61.4–9 or Ecclesiasticus 44.1–15 Psalm 15 Revelation 19.5–10 John 17.18–23	Psalms 16, **149** or **51**, 54 Daniel 3.19–end Revelation 3.14–end	Psalms 137, **138**, **143** or **38** Isaiah 3.1–15 Matthew 4.1–11
Saturday	**9 November** R/G *Margery Kempe, mystic, c.1440*	Philippians 4.10–19 Psalm 112 Luke 16.9–15	Psalms **18.31–end**, 150 or **68** Daniel 4.1–18 Revelation 4	Psalms **145** or 65, **66** Isaiah 4.2—5.7 Matthew 4.12–22

3 before Advent

		Principal Service	3rd Service	2nd Service
Sunday	10 November *R/G* **3rd Sunday before Advent** *Remembrance Sunday*	Jonah 3.1–5, 10 Psalm 62.5–end Hebrews 9.24–end Mark 1.14–20	Psalm 136 Micah 4.1–5 Philippians 4.6–9	Psalms 46 [82] Isaiah 10.33—11.9 John 14.1–29 (or 23–29)
		Holy Communion	Morning Prayer	Evening Prayer
Monday	11 November *Rw/Gw* Martin, bishop, c.397 (see p.81) DEL week 32	Titus 1.1–9 Psalm 24.1–6 Luke 17.1–6	Psalms 19, **20** or **71** Daniel 4.19–end Revelation 5	Psalm **34** or **72**, 75 Isaiah 5.8–24 Matthew 4.23—5.12
Tuesday	12 November *R/G*	Titus 2.1–8, 11–14 Psalm 37.3–5, 30–32 Luke 17.7–10	Psalms 21, 24 or **73** Daniel 5.1–12 Revelation 6	Psalms 36, **40** or **74** Isaiah 5.25–end Matthew 5.13–20
Wednesday	13 November *Rw/Gw* Charles Simeon, priest, evangelical divine, 1836 (see p.81)	Titus 3.1–7 Psalm 23 Luke 17.11–19	Psalms **23**, 25 or **77** Daniel 5.13–end Revelation 7.1–4, 9–end	Psalm **37** or 119.81–104 Isaiah 6 Matthew 5.21–37
Thursday	14 November *R/G* *Samuel Seabury, bishop, 1796*	Philemon 7–20 Psalm 146.4–end Luke 17.20–25	Psalms 26, 27 or **78**.1–39* Daniel 6 Revelation 8	Psalms 42, 43 or **78.40–end*** Isaiah 7.1–17 Matthew 5.38–end
Friday	15 November *R/G*	2 John 4–9 Psalm 119.1–8 Luke 17.26–end	Psalms 28, **32** or **55** Daniel 7.1–14 Revelation 9.1–12	Psalm 31 or **69** Isaiah 8.1–15 Matthew 6.1–18
Saturday	16 November *Rw/Gw* Margaret, queen, philanthropist, 1093 (see p.83) *Edmund Rich, archbishop, 1240*	3 John 5–8 Psalm 112 Luke 18.1–8	Psalm **33** or **76**, 79 Daniel 7.15–end Revelation 9.13–end	Psalms 84, **86** or 81, **84** Isaiah 8.16—9.7 Matthew 6.19–end

		Principal Service	3rd Service	2nd Service
Sunday	**17 November** *R/G* **2nd Sunday before Advent**	Daniel 12.1–3 Psalm 16 Hebrews 10.11–14 [15–18] 19–25 Mark 13.1–8	Psalm 96 1 Samuel 9.27—10.2a; 10.17–26 Matthew 13.31–35	Psalm 95 Daniel 3 (or 3.13–end) Matthew 13.24–30, 36–43
		Holy Communion	*Morning Prayer*	*Evening Prayer*
Monday	**18 November** *Rw/Gw* Elizabeth, princess, philanthropist, 1231 (see p.83) DEL week 33	Revelation 1.1–4, 2.1–5 Psalm 1 Luke 18.35–end	Psalms 46, 47 or 80, 82 Daniel 8.1–14 Revelation 10	Psalms 70, 71 or **85**, 86 Isaiah 9.8—10.4 Matthew 7.1–12
Tuesday	**19 November** *Rw/Gw* Hilda, abbess, 680 (see p.82) *Mechtild, béguine, mystic, 1280*	Revelation 3.1–6; 14–end Psalm 15 Luke 19.1–10	Psalms 48, 52 or 87, **89.1–18** Daniel 8.15–end Revelation 11.1–14	Psalms **67**, 72 or **89.19–end** Isaiah 10.5–19 Matthew 7.13–end
Wednesday	**20 November** *R/Gr* Edmund, king, martyr, 870 (see p.79) *Priscilla Lydia Sellon, a restorer of the* *religious life in the Church of England, 1876*	Revelation 4 Psalm 150 Luke 19.11–28	Psalms **56**, 57 or 119.**105–128** Daniel 9.1–19 Revelation 11.15–end	Psalms 73 or **91**, 93 Isaiah 10.20–32 Matthew 8.1–13
Thursday	**21 November** *R/G*	Revelation 5.1–10 Psalm 149.1–5 Luke 19.41–44	Psalms 61, **62** or 90, **92** Daniel 9.20–end Revelation 12	Psalms 74, 76 or **94** Isaiah 10.33—11.9 Matthew 8.14–22
Friday	**22 November** *R/G* *Cecilia, martyr, c.230*	Revelation 10.8–end Psalm 119.65–72 Luke 19.45–end	Psalms **63**, 65 or **88** (95) Daniel 10.1—11.1 Revelation 13.1–10	Psalm 77 or **102** Isaiah 11.10—end of 12 Matthew 8.23–end
Saturday	**23 November** *R/Gr* Clement, bishop, martyr, c.100 (see p.79)	Revelation 11.4–12 Psalm 144.1–9 Luke 20.27–40	Psalm 78.**1–39** or 96, **97**, 100 Daniel 12 Revelation 13.11–end	Psalm 78.**40–end** or **104** Isaiah 13.1–13 Matthew 9.1–17 *or:* 1st EP of Christ the King: Psalms 99, 100; Isaiah 10.33—11.9; 1 Timothy 6.11–16

Christ the King / Sunday next before Advent

			Principal Service	3rd Service	2nd Service
Sunday	**24 November** **Christ the King** *Sunday next before Advent*	R/W	Daniel 7.9–10, 13–14 Psalm 93 Revelation 1.4b–8 John 18.33–37	MP Psalms 29, 110 Isaiah 32.1–8 Revelation 3.7–end	EP Psalm 72 [or 72.1–7] Daniel 5 John 6.1–15
			Holy Communion	**Morning Prayer**	**Evening Prayer**
Monday	**25 November** *Catherine, martyr, 4th cent.* *Isaac Watts, hymn writer, 1748* DEL week 34	R/G	Revelation 14.1–5 Psalm 24.1–6 Luke 21.1–4	Psalms 92, **96** or **98**, 99, 101 Isaiah 40.1–11 Revelation 14.1–13	Psalms 80, 81 or **105*** (or 103) Isaiah 14.3–20 Matthew 9.18–34
Tuesday	**26 November**	R/G	Revelation 14.14–19 Psalm 96 Luke 21.5–11	Psalms **97**, 98, 100 or **106*** (or 103) Isaiah 40.12–26 Revelation 14.14—end of 15	Psalms 99, **101** or **107*** Isaiah 17 Matthew 9.35—10.15
Wednesday	**27 November**	R/G	Revelation 15.1–4 Psalm 98 Luke 21.12–19	Psalms 110, 111, **112** or 110, **111**, 112 Isaiah 40.27—41.7 Revelation 16.1–11	Psalms 121, **122**, 123, 124 or **119.129–152** Isaiah 19 Matthew 10.16–33
Thursday	**28 November**	R/G	Revelation 18.1–2, 21–23, 19.1–3, 9 Psalm 100 Luke 21.20–28	Psalms **125**, 126, 127, 128 or 113, **115** Isaiah 41.8–20 Revelation 16.12–end	Psalms 131, 132, **133** or 114, **116**, 117 Isaiah 21.1–12 Matthew 10.34—11.1
Friday	**29 November** *Day of Intercession and Thanksgiving* *for the Missionary Work of the Church*	R/G	Revelation 20.1–4, 11—21.2 Psalm 84.1–6 Luke 21.29–33	Psalm 139 or **139** Isaiah 41.21—42.9 Revelation 17	Psalms **146**, 147 or **130**, **131**, 137 Isaiah 22.1–14 Matthew 11.2–19 or: 1st EP of Andrew the Apostle: Psalm **48**; Isaiah **49**.1–9a; 1 Corinthians 4.9–16
			Principal Service	**3rd Service**	**2nd Service**
Saturday	**30 November** Andrew the Apostle	R	Isaiah 52.7–10 Psalm 19.1–6 Romans 10.12–18 Matthew 4.18–22	MP Psalms 47, 147.1–12 Ezekiel 47.1–12 or Ecclesiasticus 14.20–end John 12.20–32	EP Psalms 87, 96 Zechariah 8.20–end John 1.35–42

¶   *Additional Weekday Lectionary*

This Additional Weekday Lectionary provides two readings for each day of the year, except for Sundays, Principal Feasts and other Principal Holy Days, Holy Week and Festivals (for which the readings provided in the main body of this lectionary are used). The readings for 'first evensongs' in the main body of the lectionary are used on the eves of Principal Feasts and may be used on the eves of Festivals. This lectionary is intended particularly for use in those places of worship that attract occasional rather than daily worshippers, and can be used either at Morning or Evening Prayer. Psalmody is not provided and should be taken from the daily provision earlier in this volume.

	3 December – Advent 1		
Monday	4 December	Malachi 3.1–6	Matthew 3.1–6
Tuesday	5 December	Zephaniah 3.14–end	I Thessalonians 4.13–end
Wednesday	6 December	Isaiah 65.17—66.2	Matthew 24.1–14
Thursday	7 December	Micah 5.2–5a	John 3.16–21
Friday	8 December	Isaiah 66.18–end	Luke 13.22–30
Saturday	9 December	Micah 7.8–15	Romans 15.30—16.7, 25–end

	10 December – Advent 2		
Monday	11 December	Jeremiah 7.1–11	Philippians 4.4–9
Tuesday	12 December	Daniel 7.9–14	Matthew 24.15–28
Wednesday	13 December	Amos 9.11–end	Romans 13.8–14
Thursday	14 December	Jeremiah 23.5–8	Mark 11.1–11
Friday	15 December	Jeremiah 33.14–22	Luke 21.25–36
Saturday	16 December	Zechariah 14.4–11	Revelation 22.1–7

	17 December – Advent 3		
Monday	18 December	Exodus 3.1–6	Acts 7.20–36
Tuesday	19 December	Isaiah 11.1–9	Romans 15.7–13
Wednesday	20 December	Isaiah 22.21–23	Revelation 3.7–13
Thursday	21 December	Numbers 24.15b–19	Revelation 22.10–21
Friday	22 December	Jeremiah 30.7–11a	Acts 4.1–12
Saturday	23 December	Isaiah 7.10–15	Matthew 1.18–23

	24 December – Advent 4		
Monday	25 December	Christmas Day – see p.13	
Tuesday	26 December	Stephen, deacon, first martyr – see p.13	
Wednesday	27 December	John, Apostle and Evangelist – see p.13	
Thursday	28 December	The Holy Innocents – see p.13	
Friday	29 December	Micah 1.1–4; 2.12–13	Luke 2.1–7
Saturday	30 December	Isaiah 9.2–7	John 8.12–20

	31 December – Christmas 1		
Monday	1 January	Naming and Circumcision of Jesus – see p.14	
Tuesday	2 January	Isaiah 66.6–14	Matthew 12.46–50
Wednesday	3 January	Deuteronomy 6.4–15	John 10.31–end
Thursday	4 January	Isaiah 63.7–16	Galatians 3.23—4.7

	5 January – 8 January		
		If The Epiphany is celebrated on Saturday 6 January:	
Friday	5 January	*At Evening Prayer the readings for the Eve of the Epiphany are used.*	
		At other services, the following readings are used:	
		Isaiah 12	2 Corinthians 2.12–end
Saturday	6 January	The Epiphany – see p.15	
Sunday	7 January	The Baptism of Christ– see p.15	
Monday	8 January	Isaiah 41.14–20	John 1.29–34
		If, for pastoral reasons, The Epiphany is celebrated on Sunday 7 January:	
Friday	5 January	Isaiah 12	2 Corinthians 2.12–end
Saturday	6 January	*At Evening Prayer the readings for the Eve of the Epiphany are used.*	
		At other services, the following readings are used:	
		Genesis 25.19–end	Ephesians 1.1–6
Sunday	7 January	The Epiphany – see p.16	
Monday	8 January	The Baptism of Christ transferred – see p.16	

Tuesday	9 January	Exodus 17.1–7	Acts 8.26–end
Wednesday	10 January	Exodus 15.1–19	Colossians 2.8–15
Thursday	11 January	Zechariah 6.9–15	1 Peter 2.4–10
Friday	12 January	Isaiah 51.7–16	Galatians 6.14–18
Saturday	13 January	Leviticus 16.11–22	Hebrews 10.19–25

Monday	15 January	1 Kings 17.8–16	Mark 8.1–10
Tuesday	16 January	1 Kings 19.1–9a	Mark 1.9–15
Wednesday	17 January	1 Kings 19.9b–18	Mark 9.2–13
Thursday	18 January	Leviticus 11.1–8, 13–19, 41–45	Acts 10.9–16
Friday	19 January	Isaiah 49.8–13	Acts 10.34–43
Saturday	20 January	Genesis 35.1–15	Acts 10.44–end

Monday	22 January	Ezekiel 37.15–end	John 17.1–19
Tuesday	23 January	Ezekiel 20.39–44	John 17.20–end
Wednesday	24 January	Nehemiah 2.1–10	Romans 12.1–8
		or 1st EP of the Conversion of Paul	
Thursday	25 January	Conversion of Paul – see p.19	
Friday	26 January	Leviticus 19.9–28	Romans 15.1–7
Saturday	27 January	Jeremiah 33.1–11	1 Peter 5.5b–end
		If, for pastoral reasons, the Presentation of Christ *is celebrated on Sunday 28 January the readings for the Eve of the Presentation are used at Evening Prayer.*	

Monday	29 January	Jonah 3	2 Corinthians 5.11–21
Tuesday	30 January	Proverbs 4.10–end	Matthew 5.13–20
Wednesday	31 January	Isaiah 61.1–9	Luke 7.18–30
Thursday	1 February	Isaiah 52.1–12	Matthew 10.1–15
		If the Presentation of Christ *is celebrated on Friday 2 February the readings for the Eve of the Presentation are used at Evening Prayer.*	
Friday	2 February	Presentation of Christ – see p.20	
		or, if, for pastoral reasons, the Presentation of Christ *is celebrated on Sunday 28 January:*	
		Isaiah 56.1–8	Matthew 28.16–end
Saturday	3 February	Habakkuk 2.1–4	Revelation 14.1–7

Monday	5 February	Isaiah 61.1–9	Mark 6.1–13
Tuesday	6 February	Isaiah 52.1–10	Romans 10.5–21
Wednesday	7 February	Isaiah 52.13–53.6	Romans 15.14–21
Thursday	8 February	Isaiah 53.4–12	2 Corinthians 4.1–10
Friday	9 February	Zechariah 8.16–end	Matthew 10.1–15
Saturday	10 February	Jeremiah 1.4–10	Matthew 10.16–22

Monday	12 February	2 Kings 2.13–22	3 John
Tuesday	13 February	Judges 14.5–17	Revelation 10.4–11
Wednesday	14 February	Ash Wednesday – see p.23	
Thursday	15 February	Genesis 2.7–end	Hebrews 2.5–end
Friday	16 February	Genesis 4.1–12	Hebrews 4.12–end
Saturday	17 February	2 Kings 22.11–end	Hebrews 5.1–10

Monday	19 February	Genesis 6.11–end; 7.11–16	Luke 4.14–21
Tuesday	20 February	Deuteronomy 31.7–13	1 John 3.1–10
Wednesday	21 February	Genesis 11.1–9	Matthew 24.15–28
Thursday	22 February	Genesis 13.1–13	1 Peter 2.13–end
Friday	23 February	Genesis 21.1–8	Luke 9.18–27
Saturday	24 February	Genesis 32.22–32	2 Peter 1.10–end

Monday	**26 February**	I Chronicles 21.1–17	I John 2.1–8
Tuesday	**27 February**	Zechariah 3	2 Peter 2.1–10*a*
Wednesday	**28 February**	Job 1.1–22	Luke 21.34—22.6
Thursday	**29 February**	2 Chronicles 29.1–11	Mark 11.15–19
Friday	**1 March**	Exodus 19.1–9*a*	I Peter 1.1–9
Saturday	**2 March**	Exodus 19.9*b*–19	Acts 7.44–50

3 March – Lent 3

Monday	**4 March**	Joshua 4.1–13	Luke 9.1–11
Tuesday	**5 March**	Exodus 15.22–27	Hebrews 10.32–end
Wednesday	**6 March**	Genesis 9.8–17	I Peter 3.18–end
Thursday	**7 March**	Daniel 12.5–end	Mark 13.21–end
Friday	**8 March**	Numbers 20.1–13	I Corinthians 10.23–end
Saturday	**9 March**	Isaiah 43.14–end	Hebrews 3.1–15

10 March – Lent 4

Monday	**11 March**	2 Kings 24.18—25.7	I Corinthians 15.20–34
Tuesday	**12 March**	Jeremiah 13.12–19	Acts 13.26–35
Wednesday	**13 March**	Jeremiah 13.20–27	I Peter 1.17—2.3
Thursday	**14 March**	Jeremiah 22.11–19	Luke 11.37–52
Friday	**15 March**	Jeremiah 17.1–14	Luke 6.17–26
Saturday	**16 March**	Ezra 1	2 Corinthians 1.12–19

17 March – Lent 5

Monday	**18 March**	Joel 2.12–17 or 1st EP of Joseph of Nazareth	2 John
Tuesday	**19 March**	Joseph of Nazareth – **see p.28**	
Wednesday	**20 March**	Job 36.1–12	John 14.1–14
Thursday	**21 March**	Jeremiah 9.17–22	Luke 13.31–35
Friday	**22 March**	Lamentations 5.1–3,19–22	John 12.20–26
Saturday	**23 March**	Job 17.6–end	John 12.27–36

From the Monday of Holy Week until Easter Eve the seasonal lectionary is used: see pp.29–30.

31 March – Easter

Monday	**1 April**	Isaiah 54.1–14	Romans 1.1–7
Tuesday	**2 April**	Isaiah 51.1–11	John 5.19–29
Wednesday	**3 April**	Isaiah 26.1–19	John 20.1–10
Thursday	**4 April**	Isaiah 43.14–21	Revelation 1.4–end
Friday	**5 April**	Isaiah 42.10–17	I Thessalonians 5.1–11
Saturday	**6 April**	Job 14.1–14	John 21.1–14

7 April – Easter 2

Monday	**8 April**	Annunciation of Our Lord to the Blessed Virgin Mary transferred – see p.32	
Tuesday	**9 April**	Proverbs 8.1–11	Acts 16.6–15
Wednesday	**10 April**	Hosea 5.15—6.6	I Corinthians 15.1–11
Thursday	**11 April**	Jonah 2	Mark 4.35–end
Friday	**12 April**	Genesis 6.9–end	I Peter 3.8–end
Saturday	**13 April**	I Samuel 2.1–8	Matthew 28.8–15

14 April – Easter 3

Monday	**15 April**	Exodus 24.1–11	Revelation 5
Tuesday	**16 April**	Leviticus 19.9–18, 32–end	Matthew 5.38–end
Wednesday	**17 April**	Genesis 3.8–21	I Corinthians 15.12–28
Thursday	**18 April**	Isaiah 33.13–22	Mark 6.47–end
Friday	**19 April**	Nehemiah 9.6–17	Romans 5.12–end
Saturday	**20 April**	Isaiah 61.10—62.5	Luke 24.1–12

Monday	**22 April**	Jeremiah 31.10–17	Revelation 7.9–end
		or 1st EP of George	
Tuesday	**23 April**	George, martyr, patron of England – see p.34	
Wednesday	**24 April**	Genesis 2.4b–9	1 Corinthians 15.35–49
		or 1st EP of Mark the Evangelist	
Thursday	**25 April**	Mark the Evangelist – see p.34	
Friday	**26 April**	Ecclesiastes 12.1–8	Romans 6.1–11
Saturday	**27 April**	1 Chronicles 29.10–13	Luke 24.13–35

Monday	**29 April**	Genesis 15.1–18	Romans 4.13–end
Tuesday	**30 April**	Deuteronomy 8.1–10	Matthew 6.19–end
		or 1st EP of Philip and James, Apostles	
Wednesday	**1 May**	Philip and James, Apostles – see p.35	
Thursday	**2 May**	Exodus 3.1–15	Mark 12.18–27
Friday	**3 May**	Ezekiel 36.33–end	Romans 8.1–11
Saturday	**4 May**	Isaiah 38.9–20	Luke 24.33–end

Monday	**6 May**	Proverbs 4.1–13	Philippians 2.1–11
Tuesday	**7 May**	Isaiah 32.12–end	Romans 5.1–11
Wednesday	**8 May**	At Evening Prayer the readings for the Eve of Ascension Day are used.	
		At other services, the following readings are used:	
		Isaiah 43.1–13	Titus 2.11—3.8
Thursday	**9 May**	Ascension Day – see p.36	
Friday	**10 May**	Exodus 35.30—36.1	Galatians 5.13–end
Saturday	**11 May**	Numbers 11.16–17, 24–29	1 Corinthians 2

Monday	**13 May**	Numbers 27.15–end	1 Corinthians 3
		or 1st EP of Matthias the Apostle	
Tuesday	**14 May**	Matthias the Apostle – see p.37	
Wednesday	**15 May**	1 Kings 19.1–18	Matthew 3.13–end
Thursday	**16 May**	Ezekiel 11.14–20	Matthew 9.35—10.20
Friday	**17 May**	Ezekiel 36.22–28	Matthew 12.22–32
Saturday	**18 May**	At Evening Prayer the readings for the Eve of Pentecost are used.	
		At other services, the following readings are used:	
		Micah 3.1–8	Ephesians 6.10–20

Monday	**20 May**	Genesis 12.1–9	Romans 4.13–end
Tuesday	**21 May**	Genesis 13.1–12	Romans 12.9–end
Wednesday	**22 May**	Genesis 15	Romans 4.1–8
Thursday	**23 May**	Genesis 22.1–18	Hebrews 11.8–19
Friday	**24 May**	Isaiah 51.1–8	John 8.48–end
Saturday	**25 May**	At Evening Prayer the readings for the Eve of Trinity Sunday are used.	
		At other services, the following readings are used:	
		Ecclesiasticus 44.19–23	James 2.14–26
		or Joshua 2.1–15	

Monday	**27 May**	Exodus 2.1–10	Hebrews 11.23–31
Tuesday	**28 May**	Exodus 2.11–end	Acts 7.17–29
Wednesday	**29 May**	Exodus 3.1–12	Acts 7.30–38
		or 1st EP of Corpus Christi	
Thursday	**30 May**	Day of Thanksgiving for the Institution of Holy Communion	
		(Corpus Christi) – see p.39	
		or, where Corpus Christi is not celebrated as Festival:	
		Exodus 6.1–13	John 9.24–38
		or 1st EP of the Visit of the Blessed Virgin Mary to Elizabeth	
Friday	**31 May**	Visit of the Blessed Virgin Mary to Elizabeth – see p.40	
Saturday	**1 June**	Exodus 34.27–end	2 Corinthians 3.7–end

Monday	3 June	Genesis 37.1–11	Romans 11.9–21
Tuesday	4 June	Genesis 41.15–40	Mark 13.1–13
Wednesday	5 June	Genesis 42.17–end	Matthew 18.1–14
Thursday	6 June	Genesis 45.1–15	Acts 7.9–16
Friday	7 June	Genesis 47.1–12	I Thessalonians 5.12–end
Saturday	8 June	Genesis 50.4–21	Luke 15.11–end

Monday	10 June	Isaiah 32	James 3.13–end
		or 1st EP of Barnabas the Apostle	
Tuesday	11 June	Barnabas the Apostle – see p.42	
Wednesday	12 June	Judges 6.1–16	Matthew 5.13–24
Thursday	13 June	Jeremiah 6.9–15	I Timothy 2.1–6
Friday	14 June	I Samuel 16.14–end	John 14.15–end
Saturday	15 June	Isaiah 6.1–9	Revelation 19.9–end

Monday	17 June	Exodus 13.13b–end	Luke 15.1–10
Tuesday	18 June	Proverbs 1.20–end	James 5.13–end
Wednesday	19 June	Isaiah 5.8–24	James 1.17–25
Thursday	20 June	Isaiah 57.14–end	John 13.1–17
Friday	21 June	Jeremiah 15.15–end	Luke 16.19–31
Saturday	22 June	Isaiah 25.1–9	Acts 2.22–33

Monday	24 June	Birth of John the Baptist – see p.44	
Tuesday	25 June	Proverbs 6.6–19	Luke 4.1–14
Wednesday	26 June	Isaiah 24.1–15	I Corinthians 6.1–11
Thursday	27 June	Job 7	Matthew 7 21–29
Friday	28 June	Jeremiah 20.7–end	Matthew 27.27–44
		or 1st EP of Peter and Paul, Apostles (or Peter the Apostle)	
Saturday	29 June	Peter and Paul, Apostles (or Peter the Apostle) – see p.44	

Monday	1 July	Exodus 32.1–14	Colossians 3.1–11
Tuesday	2 July	Proverbs 9.1–12	2 Thessalonians 2.13—3.5
		or 1st EP of Thomas the Apostle	
Wednesday	3 July	Thomas the Apostle – see p.45	
Thursday	4 July	Jeremiah 8.18—9.6	John 13.21–35
Friday	5 July	2 Samuel 5.1–12	Matthew 27.45–56
Saturday	6 July	Hosea 11.1–11	Matthew 28.1–7

Monday	8 July	Exodus 40.1–16	Luke 14.15–24
Tuesday	9 July	Proverbs 11.1–12	Mark 12.38–44
Wednesday	10 July	Isaiah 33.2–10	Philippians 1.1–11
Thursday	11 July	Job 38	Luke 18.1–14
Friday	12 July	Job 42.1–6	John 3.1–15
Saturday	13 July	Ecclesiastes 9.1–11	Hebrews 1.1–9

Monday	15 July	Numbers 23.1–12	I Corinthians 1.10–17
Tuesday	16 July	Proverbs 12.1–12	Galatians 3.1–14
Wednesday	17 July	Isaiah 49.8–13	2 Corinthians 8.1–11
Thursday	18 July	Hosea 14	John 15.1–17
Friday	19 July	2 Samuel 18.18–end	Matthew 27.57–66
Saturday	20 July	Isaiah 55.1–7	Mark 16.1–8

Monday	22 July	Mary Magdalene – see p.48	
Tuesday	23 July	Proverbs 12.13–end	John 1.43–51
Wednesday	24 July	Isaiah 55.8–end	2 Timothy 2.8–19
		or 1st EP of James the Apostle	
Thursday	25 July	James the Apostle – see p.48	
Friday	26 July	Jeremiah 14.1–9	Luke 8.4–15
Saturday	27 July	Ecclesiastes 5.10–19	I Timothy 6.6–16

Monday	29 July	Joshua 1.1–9	1 Corinthians 9.19–end
Tuesday	30 July	Proverbs 15.1–11	Galatians 2.15–end
Wednesday	31 July	Isaiah 49.1–7	1 John 1
Thursday	1 August	Proverbs 27.1–12	John 15.12–27
Friday	2 August	Isaiah 59.8–end	Mark 15.6–20
Saturday	3 August	Zechariah 7.8—8.8	Luke 20.27–40

Monday	5 August	Judges 13.1–23	Luke 10.38–42
		or 1st EP of the Transfiguration of Our Lord	
Tuesday	6 August	Transfiguration of Our Lord – see p.50	
Wednesday	7 August	Isaiah 45.1–7	Ephesians 4.1–16
Thursday	8 August	Jeremiah 16.1–15	Luke 12.35–48
Friday	9 August	Jeremiah 18.1–11	Hebrews 1.1–9
Saturday	10 August	Jeremiah 26.1–19	Ephesians 3.1–13

Monday	12 August	Ruth 2.1–13	Luke 10.25–37
Tuesday	13 August	Proverbs 16.1–11	Philippians 3.4b–end
Wednesday	14 August	Deuteronomy 11.1–21	2 Corinthians 9.6–end
		or 1st EP of The Blessed Virgin Mary	
Thursday	15 August	The Blessed Virgin Mary – see p.51	
Friday	16 August	Obadiah 1–10	John 19.1–16
Saturday	17 August	2 Kings 2.11–14	Luke 24.36–end

Monday	19 August	1 Samuel 17.32–50	Matthew 8.14–22
Tuesday	20 August	Proverbs 17.1–15	Luke 7.1–17
Wednesday	21 August	Jeremiah 5.20–end	2 Peter 3.8–end
Thursday	22 August	Daniel 2.1–23	Luke 10.1–20
Friday	23 August	Daniel 3.1–28	Revelation 15
		or 1st EP of Bartholomew the Apostle	
Saturday	24 August	Bartholomew the Apostle – see p.52	

Monday	26 August	2 Samuel 7.4–17	2 Corinthians 5.1–10
Tuesday	27 August	Proverbs 18.10–21	Romans 14.10–end
Wednesday	28 August	Judges 4.1–10	Romans 1.8–17
Thursday	29 August	Isaiah 49.14–end	John 16.16–24
Friday	30 August	Job 9.1–24	Mark 15.21–32
Saturday	31 August	Exodus 19.1–9	John 20.11–18

Monday	2 September	Haggai 1	Mark 7.9–23
Tuesday	3 September	Proverbs 21.1–18	Mark 6.30–44
Wednesday	4 September	Hosea 11.1–11	1 John 4.9–end
Thursday	5 September	Lamentations 3.34–48	Romans 7.14–end
Friday	6 September	1 Kings 19.4–18	1 Thessalonians 3
Saturday	7 September	Ecclesiasticus 4.11–28	2 Timothy 3.10–end
		or Deuteronomy 29.2–15	

Monday	9 September	Wisdom 6.12–21 or Job 12.1–16	Matthew 15.1–9
Tuesday	10 September	Proverbs 8.1–11	Luke 6.39–end
Wednesday	11 September	Proverbs 2.1–15	Colossians 1.9–20
Thursday	12 September	Baruch 3.14–end or Genesis 1.1–13	John 1.1–18
Friday	13 September	Ecclesiasticus 1.1–20	1 Corinthians 1.18–end
		or Deuteronomy 7.7–16	
		or 1st EP of Holy Cross Day	
Saturday	14 September	Holy Cross Day – see p.55	

Monday	16 September	Genesis 21.1–13	Luke 1.26–38
Tuesday	17 September	Ruth 4.7–17	Luke 2.25–38
Wednesday	18 September	2 Kings 4.1–7	John 2.1–11
Thursday	19 September	2 Kings 4.25b–37	Mark 3.19b–35
Friday	20 September	Judith 8.9–17, 28–36 or Ruth 1.1–18 or 1st EP of Matthew the Apostle	John 19.25b–30
Saturday	21 September	Matthew the Apostle – see p.56	

Monday	23 September	Exodus 19.16–end	Hebrews 12.18–end
Tuesday	24 September	1 Chronicles 16.1–13	Revelation 11.15–end
Wednesday	25 September	1 Chronicles 29.10–19	Colossians 3.12–17
Thursday	26 September	Nehemiah 8.1–12	1 Corinthians 14.1–12
Friday	27 September	Isaiah 1.10–17	Mark 12.28–34
Saturday	28 September	Daniel 6.6–23 or 1st EP of Michael and All Angels	Revelation 12.7–12

Monday	30 September	2 Samuel 22.4–7, 17–20 or Michael and All Angels (transferred from 29 September) – see p.58	Hebrews 7.26—8.6
Tuesday	1 October	Proverbs 22.17–end	2 Corinthians 12.1–10
Wednesday	2 October	Hosea 14	James 2.14–26
Thursday	3 October	Isaiah 24.1–15	John 16.25–33
Friday	4 October	Jeremiah 14.1–9	Luke 23.44–56
Saturday	5 October	Zechariah 8.14–end	John 20.19–end

Monday	7 October	1 Kings 3.3–14	1 Timothy 3.14—4.8
Tuesday	8 October	Proverbs 27.11–end	Galatians 6.1–10
Wednesday	9 October	Isaiah 51.1–6	2 Corinthians 1.1–11
Thursday	10 October	Ecclesiasticus 18.1–14 or Job 26	1 Corinthians 11.17–end
Friday	11 October	Ecclesiasticus 28.2–12 or Job 19.21–end	Mark 15.33–47
Saturday	12 October	Isaiah 44.21–end	John 21.15–end

Monday	14 October	1 Kings 6.2–10	John 12.1–11
Tuesday	15 October	Proverbs 31.10–end	Luke 10.38–42
Wednesday	16 October	Jonah 1	Luke 5.1–11
Thursday	17 October	Exodus 12.1–20 or 1st EP of Luke the Evangelist	1 Thessalonians 4.1–12
Friday	18 October	Luke the Evangelist – see p.61	
Saturday	19 October	2 Samuel 7.18–end	Acts 2.22–33

Monday	21 October	1 Kings 8.22–30	John 12.12–19
Tuesday	22 October	Ecclesiastes 11	Luke 13.10–17
Wednesday	23 October	Hosea 14.1–7	2 Timothy 4.1–8
Thursday	24 October	Isaiah 49.1–7	John 19.16–25a
Friday	25 October	Proverbs 24.3–22	John 8.1–11
Saturday	26 October	Ecclesiasticus 7.8–17, 32–end or Deuteronomy 6.16–25	2 Timothy 1.1–14

Monday	28 October	Simon and Jude, Apostles – see p.63	
Tuesday	29 October	I Samuel 4.12–end	Luke 1.57–80
Wednesday	30 October	Baruch 5 or Haggai 1.1–11	Mark 1.1–11
Thursday	31 October	Isaiah 35	Matthew 11.2–19
		or 1st EP of All Saints' Day	
Friday	I November	All Saints' Day – see p.64	
		or, if All Saints' Day is celebrated on Sunday 3 November only, the	
		following readings are used:	
		2 Samuel 11.1–17	
		Matthew 14.1–12	
Saturday	2 November	Isaiah 43.15–21	Acts 19.1–10
		or 1st EP of All Saints' Day, if All Saints' Day is celebrated on	
		3 November	

Monday	4 November	Esther 3.1–11; 4.7–17	Matthew 18.1–10
Tuesday	5 November	Ezekiel 18.21–end	Matthew 18.12–20
Wednesday	6 November	Proverbs 3.27–end	Matthew 18.21–end
Thursday	7 November	Exodus 23.1–9	Matthew 19.1–15
Friday	8 November	Proverbs 3.13–18	Matthew 19.16–end
Saturday	9 November	Deuteronomy 28.1–6	Matthew 20.1–16

Monday	II November	Isaiah 40.21–end	Romans 11.25–end
Tuesday	12 November	Ezekiel 34.20–end	John 10.1–18
Wednesday	13 November	Leviticus 26.3–13	Titus 2.1–10
Thursday	14 November	Hosea 6.1–6	Matthew 9.9–13
Friday	15 November	Malachi 4	John 4.5–26
Saturday	16 November	Micah 6.6–8	Colossians 3.12–17

Monday	18 November	Micah 7.1–7	Matthew 10.24–39
Tuesday	19 November	Habakkuk 3.1–19a	I Corinthians 4.9–16
Wednesday	20 November	Zechariah 8.1–13	Mark 13.3–8
Thursday	21 November	Zechariah 10.6–end	I Peter 5.1–11
Friday	22 November	Micah 4.1–5	Luke 9.28–36
Saturday	23 November	At Evening Prayer the readings for the Eve of Christ the King may be used.	
		At other services, the following readings are used:	
		Exodus 16.1–21	John 6.3–15

Monday	25 November	Jeremiah 30.1–3, 10–17	Romans 12.9–21
Tuesday	26 November	Jeremiah 30.18–24	John 10.22–30
Wednesday	27 November	Jeremiah 31.1–9	Matthew 15.21–31
Thursday	28 November	Jeremiah 31.10–17	Matthew 16.13–end
Friday	29 November	Jeremiah 31.31–37	Hebrews 10.11–18
		or 1st EP of Andrew the Apostle	
Saturday	30 November	Andrew the Apostle – see p.69	

¶ Collects and Post Communions

All the contemporary language Collects and Post Communions, including the Additional Collects, may be found in *Common Worship: Collects and Post Communions* (Church House Publishing: London, 2004). The Additional Collects are also published separately.

The contemporary language Collects and Post Communions all appear in *Times and Seasons: President's Edition for Holy Communion*. Apart from the Additional Collects, they appear in the other Common Worship volumes as follows:

¶ President's edition: all Collects and Post Communions;
¶ *Daily Prayer*: all Collects;
¶ main volume: Collects and Post Communions for Sundays, Principal Feasts and Holy Days, and Festivals;
¶ *Festivals*: Collects and Post Communions for Festivals, Lesser Festivals, Common of the Saints and Special Occasions.

The traditional-language Collects and Post Communions all appear in the president's edition. They appear in other publications as follows:

¶ main volume: Collects and Post Communions for Sundays, Principal Feasts and Holy Days, and Festivals;
¶ separate booklet: Collects and Post Communions for Lesser Festivals, Common of the Saints and Special Occasions.

¶ Lectionary for Dedication Festival

If date not known, observe on the first Sunday in October or Last Sunday after Trinity.

Evening Prayer on the Eve
Psalm 24
2 Chronicles 7.11–16
John 4.19–29

Dedication Festival
Gold or White

	Principal Service	3rd Service	2nd Service	Psalmody
Year A	1 Kings 8.22–30 or Revelation 21.9–14 Psalm 122 Hebrews 12.18–24 Matthew 21.12–16	Haggai 2.6–9 Hebrews 10.19–25	Jeremiah 7.1–11 1 Corinthians 3.9–17 HC Luke 19.1–10	MP 48, 150 EP 132
Year B	Genesis 28.11–18 or Revelation 21.9–14 Psalm 122 1 Peter 2.1–10 John 10.22–29	Haggai 2.6–9 Hebrews 10.19–25	Jeremiah 7.1–11 Luke 19.1–10	MP 48, 150 EP 132
Year C	1 Chronicles 29.6–19 Psalm 122 Ephesians 2.19–end John 2.13–22	Haggai 2.6–9 Hebrews 10.19–25	Jeremiah 7.1–11 Luke 19.1–10	MP 48, 150 EP 132

The Blessed Virgin Mary

Genesis 3.8–15, 20; Isaiah 7.10–14; Micah 5.1–4
Psalms 45.10–17; 113; 131
Acts 1.12–14; Romans 8.18–30; Galatians 4.4–7
Luke 1.26–38; *or* 1.39–47; John 19.25–27

Martyrs

2 Chronicles 24.17–21; Isaiah 43.1–7; Jeremiah 11.18–20; Wisdom 4.10–15
Psalms 3; 11; 31.1–5; 44.18–24; 126
Romans 8.35–end; 2 Corinthians 4.7–15; 2 Timothy 2.3–7 [8–13]; Hebrews 11.32–end;
    1 Peter 4.12–end; Revelation 12.10–12*a*
Matthew 10.16–22; *or* 10.28–39; *or* 16.24–26; John 12.24–26; *or* 15.18–21

Agnes (21 Jan): *also* Revelation 7.13–end
Alban (22 June): *especially* 2 Timothy 2.3–13; John 12.24–26
Alphege (19 Apr): *also* Hebrews 5.1–4
Boniface (5 June): *also* Acts 20.24–28
Charles (30 Jan): *also* Ecclesiasticus 2.12–end; 1 Timothy 6.12–16
Clement (23 Nov): *also* Philippians 3.17—4.3; Matthew 16.13–19
Cyprian (15 Sept): *especially* 1 Peter 4.12–end; *also* Matthew 18.18–22
Edmund (20 Nov): *also* Proverbs 20.28; 21.1–4, 7
Ignatius (17 Oct): *also* Philippians 3.7–12; John 6.52–58
James Hannington (29 Oct): *especially* Matthew 10.28–39
Janani Luwum (17 Feb): *also* Ecclesiasticus 4.20–28; John 12.24–32
John Coleridge Patteson (20 Sept): *especially* 2 Chronicles 24.17–21; *also* Acts 7.55–end
Justin (1 June): *especially* John 15.18–21; *also* 1 Maccabees 2.15–22; 1 Corinthians 1.18–25
Laurence (10 Aug): *also* 2 Corinthians 9.6–10
Lucy (13 Dec): *also* Wisdom 3.1–7; 2 Corinthians 4.6–15
Oswald (5 Aug): *especially* 1 Peter 4.12–end; John 16.29–end
Perpetua, Felicity and comps (7 Mar): *especially* Revelation 12.10–12*a*; *also* Wisdom 3.1–7
Polycarp (23 Feb): *also* Revelation 2.8–11
Thomas Becket (29 Dec *or* 7 Jul): *especially* Matthew 10.28–33; *also* Ecclesiasticus 51.1–8
William Tyndale (6 Oct): *also* Proverbs 8.4–11; 2 Timothy 3.12–end

Teachers of the Faith and Spiritual Writers

1 Kings 3.[6–10] 11–14; Proverbs 4.1–9; Wisdom 7.7–10, 15–16; Ecclesiasticus 39.1–10
Psalms 19.7–10; 34.11–17; 37.31–35; 119.89–96; 119.97–104
1 Corinthians 1.18–25; *or* 2.1–10; *or* 2.9–end; Ephesians 3.8–12; 2 Timothy 4.1–8;
    Titus 2.1–8
Matthew 5.13–19; *or* 13.52–end; *or* 23.8–12; Mark 4.1–9; John 16.12–15

Ambrose (7 Dec): *also* Isaiah 41.9b–13; Luke 22.24–30
Anselm (21 Apr): *also* Wisdom 9.13–end; Romans 5.8–11
Athanasius (2 May): *also* Ecclesiasticus 4.20–28; *also* Matthew 10.24–27
Augustine of Hippo (28 Aug): *especially* Ecclesiasticus 39.1–10; *also* Romans 13.11–13
Basil and Gregory (2 Jan): *especially* 2 Timothy 4.1–8; Matthew 5.13–19
Bernard (20 Aug): *especially* Revelation 19.5–9
Catherine of Siena (29 Apr): *also* Proverbs 8.1, 6–11; John 17.12–end
Francis de Sales (24 Jan): *also* Proverbs 3.13–18; John 3.17–21
Gregory the Great (3 Sept): *also* 1 Thessalonians 2.3–8
Gregory of Nyssa and Macrina (19 July): *especially* 1 Corinthians 2.9–13;
    also Wisdom 9.13–17
Hilary (13 Jan): *also* 1 John 2.18–25; John 8.25–32
Irenaeus (28 June): *also* 2 Peter 1.16–end
Jeremy Taylor (13 Aug); *also* Titus 2.7–8, 11–14
John Bunyan (30 Aug): *also* Hebrews 12.1–2; Luke 21.21, 34–36
John Chrysostom (13 Sept): *especially* Matthew 5.13–19; *also* Jeremiah 1.4–10
John of the Cross (14 Dec): *especially* 1 Corinthians 2.1–10; *also* John 14.18–23
Leo (10 Nov): *also* 1 Peter 5.1–11
Richard Hooker (3 Nov): *especially* John 16.12–15; *also* Ecclesiasticus 44.10–15
Teresa of Avila (15 Oct): *also* Romans 8.22–27
Thomas Aquinas (28 Jan): *especially* Wisdom 7.7–10, 15–16; 1 Corinthians 2.9–end;
    John 16.12–15
William Law (10 Apr): *especially* 1 Corinthians 2.9–end; *also* Matthew 17.1–9

Bishops and Other Pastors

I Samuel 16.1, 6–13; Isaiah 6.1–8; Jeremiah 1.4–10; Ezekiel 3.16–21; Malachi 2.5–7
Psalms 1; 15; 16.5–end; 96; 110
Acts 20.28–35; I Corinthians 4.1–5; 2 Corinthians 4.1–10 [*or* 1–2, 5–7];
   or 5.14–20; I Peter 5.1–4
Matthew 11.25–end; *or* 24.42–46; John 10.11–16; *or* 15.9–17; *or* 21.15–17

Augustine of Canterbury (26 May): *also* I Thessalonians 2.2*b*–8; Matthew 13.31–33
Charles Simeon (13 Nov): *especially* Malachi 2.5–7; *also* Colossians 1.3–8; Luke 8.4–8
David (1 Mar): *also* 2 Samuel 23.1–4; Psalm 89.19–22, 24
Dunstan (19 May): *especially* Matthew 24.42–46; *also* Exodus 31.1–5
Edward King (8 Mar): *also* Hebrews 13.1–8
George Herbert (27 Feb): *especially* Malachi 2.5–7; Matthew 11.25–end;
   also Revelation 19.5–9
Hugh (17 Nov); *also* I Timothy 6.11–16
John Keble (14 July): *also* Lamentations 3.19–26; Matthew 5.1–8
John and Charles Wesley (24 May): *also* Ephesians 5.15–20
Lancelot Andrewes (25 Sept): *especially* Isaiah 6.1–8
Martin of Tours (11 Nov): *also* I Thessalonians 5.1–11; Matthew 25.34–40
Nicholas (6 Dec): *also* Isaiah 61.1–3; I Timothy 6.6–11; Mark 10.13–16
Richard (16 June): *also* John 21.15–19
Swithun (15 July): *also* James 5.7–11, 13–18
Thomas Ken (8 June): *especially* 2 Corinthians 4.1–10 [*or* 1–2, 5–7]; Matthew 24.42–46
Wulfstan (19 Jan): *especially* Matthew 24.42–46

Members of Religious Communities

1 Kings 19.9–18; Proverbs 10.27–end; Song of Solomon 8.6–7; Isaiah 61.10—62.5;
    Hosea 2.14–15, 19–20
Psalms 34.1–8; 112.1–9; 119.57–64; 123; 131
Acts 4.32–35; 2 Corinthians 10.17—11.2; Philippians 3.7–14; 1 John 2.15–17;
    Revelation 19.1, 5–9
Matthew 11.25–end; or 19.3–12; or 19.23–end; Luke 9.57–end; or 12.32–37

Aelred (12 Jan): also Ecclesiasticus 15.1–6
Alcuin (20 May): also Colossians 3.12–16; John 4.19–24
Antony (17 Jan): especially Philippians 3.7–14, also Matthew 19.16–26
Bede (25 May): also Ecclesiasticus 39.1–10
Benedict (11 July): also 1 Corinthians 3.10–11; Luke 18.18–22
Clare (11 Aug): especially Song of Solomon 8.6–7
Dominic (8 Aug): also Ecclesiasticus 39.1–10
Etheldreda (23 June): also Matthew 25.1–13
Francis of Assisi (4 Oct): also Galatians 6.14–end; Luke 12.22–34
Hilda (19 Nov): especially Isaiah 61.10—62.5
Hildegard (17 Sept): also 1 Corinthians 2.9–13; Luke 10.21–24
Julian of Norwich (8 May): also 1 Corinthians 13.8–end; Matthew 5.13–16
Vincent de Paul (27 Sept): also 1 Corinthians 1.25–end; Matthew 25.34–40

Missionaries

Isaiah 52.7–10; or 61.1–3a; Ezekiel 34.11–16; Jonah 3.1–5
Psalms 67; or 87; or 97; or 100; or 117
Acts 2.14, 22–36; or 13.46–49; or 16.6–10; or 26.19–23; Romans 15.17–21;
    2 Corinthians 5.11—6.2
Matthew 9.35–end; or 28.16–end; Mark 16.15–20; Luke 5.1–11; or 10.1–9

Aidan (31 Aug): also 1 Corinthians 9.16–19
Anskar (3 Feb): especially Isaiah 52.7–10; also Romans 10.11–15
Chad (2 Mar or 26 Oct): also 1 Timothy 6.11b–16
Columba (9 June): also Titus 2.11–end
Cuthbert (20 Mar or 4 Sept): especially Ezekiel 34.11–16; also Matthew 18.12–14
Cyril and Methodius (14 Feb): especially Isaiah 52.7–10; also Romans 10.11–15
Henry Martyn (19 Oct): especially Mark 16.15–end; also Isaiah 55.6–11
Ninian (16 Sept): especially Acts 13.46–49; Mark 16.15–end
Patrick (17 Mar): also Psalm 91.1–4, 13–end; Luke 10.1–12, 17–20
Paulinus (10 Oct); especially Matthew 28.16–end
Wilfrid (12 Oct): especially Luke 5.1–11; also 1 Corinthians 1.18–25
Willibrord (7 Nov): especially Isaiah 52.7–10; Matthew 28.16–end

Any Saint

General

Genesis 12.1–4; Proverbs 8.1–11; Micah 6.6–8; Ecclesiasticus 2.7–13 [14–end]
Psalms 32; 33.1–5; 119.1–8; 139.1–4 [5–12]; 145.8–14
Ephesians 3.14–19; *or* 6.11–18; Hebrews 13.7–8, 15–16; James 2.14–17;
    1 John 4.7–16; Revelation 21.[1–4] 5–7
Matthew 19.16–21; *or* 25.1–13; *or* 25.14–30; John 15.1–8; *or* 17.20–end

Christian rulers

1 Samuel 16.1–13*a*; 1 Kings 3.3–14
Psalms 72.1–7; 99
1 Timothy 2.1–6
Mark 10.42–45; Luke 14.27–33

Alfred the Great (26 Oct): *also* 2 Samuel 23.1–5; John 18.33–37
Edward the Confessor (13 Oct): *also* 2 Samuel 23.1–5; 1 John 4.13–16
Margaret of Scotland (16 Nov): *also* Proverbs 31.10–12, 20, 26–end;
    1 Corinthians 12.13—13.3; Matthew 25.34–end

Those working for the poor and underprivileged

Isaiah 58.6–11
Psalms 82; 146.5–10
Hebrews 13.1–3; 1 John 3.14–18
Matthew 5.1–12; *or* 25.31–end

Elizabeth of Hungary (18 Nov): *especially* Matthew 25.31–end; *also* Proverbs 31.10–end
Josephine Butler (30 May): *especially* Isaiah 58.6–11; *also* 1 John 3.18–23; Matthew 9.10–13
William Wilberforce, Olaudah Equiano and Thomas Clarkson (30 July): *also* Job 31.16–23;
    Galatians 3.26–end, 4.6–7; Luke 4.16–21

Men and women of learning

Proverbs 8.22–31; Ecclesiasticus 44.1–15
Psalms 36.5–10; 49.1–4
Philippians 4.7–8
Matthew 13.44–46, 52; John 7.14–18

Those whose holiness was revealed in marriage and family life

Proverbs 31.10–13, 19–20, 30–end; Tobit 8.4–7
Psalms 127; 128
1 Peter 3.1–9
Mark 3.31–end; Luke 10.38–end

Mary Sumner (9 Aug): *also* Hebrews 13.1–5
Monica (27 Aug): *also* Ecclesiasticus 26.1–3, 13–16

The Guidance of the Holy Spirit

Proverbs 24.3–7; Isaiah 30.15–21; Wisdom 9.13–17
Psalms 25.1–9; 104.26–33; 143.8–10
Acts 15.23–29; Romans 8:22–27; 1 Corinthians 12.4–13
Luke 14.27–33; John 14.23–26; *or* 16.13–15

Rogation Days
(6–8 May in 2024)

Deuteronomy 8.1–10; 1 Kings 8.35–40; Job 28.1–11
Psalms 104.21–30; 107.1–9; 121
Philippians 4.4–7; 2 Thessalonians 3.6–13; 1 John 5.12–15
Matthew 6.1–15; Mark 11.22–24; Luke 11.5–13

Harvest Thanksgiving

Year A	Year B	Year C
Deuteronomy 8.7–18 *or* 28.1–14	Joel 2.21–27	Deuteronomy 26.1–11
Psalm 65	Psalm 126	Psalm 100
2 Corinthians 9.6–end	1 Timothy 2.1–7; *or* 6.6–10	Philippians 4.4–9
Luke 12.16–30; *or* 17.11–19	Matthew 6.25–33	*or* Revelation 14.14–18
		John 6.25–35

Mission and Evangelism

Isaiah 49.1–6; *or* 52.7–10; Micah 4.1–5
Psalms 2; 46; 67
Acts 17.10–end; 2 Corinthians 5.14–6.2; Ephesians 2.13–end
Matthew 5.13–16; *or* 28.16–end; John 17.20–end

The Unity of the Church

Jeremiah 33.6–9a; Ezekiel 36.23–28; Zephaniah 3.16–end
Psalms 100; 122; 133
Ephesians 4.1–6; Colossians 3.9–17; 1 John 4.9–15
Matthew 18.19–22; John 11.45–52; *or* 17.11b–23

The Peace of the World

Isaiah 9.1–6; *or* 57.15–19; Micah 4.1–5
Psalms 40.14–17; 72.1–7; 85.8–13
Philippians 4.6–9; 1 Timothy 2.1–6; James 3.13–18
Matthew 5.43–end; John 14.23–29; *or* 15.9–17

Social Justice and Responsibility

Isaiah 32.15–end; Amos 5.21–24; or 8.4–7; Acts 5.1–11
Psalms 31.21–24; 85.1–7; 146.5–10
Colossians 3.12–15; James 2.1–4
Matthew 5.1–12; or 25.31–end; Luke 16.19–end

Ministry, including Ember Days
(See page 7)

Numbers 11.16–17, 24–29; or 27.15–end; 1 Samuel 16.1–13a; Isaiah 6.1–8;
    or 61.1–3; Jeremiah 1.4–10
Psalms 40.8–13; 84.8–12; 89.19–25; 101.1–5, 7; 122
Acts 20.28–35; 1 Corinthians 3.3–11; Ephesians 4.4–16; Philippians 3.7–14
Luke 4.16–21; or 12.35–43; or 22.24–27; John 4.31–38; or 15.5–17

In Time of Trouble

Genesis 9.8–17; Job 1.13–end; Isaiah 38.6–11
Psalms 86.1–7; 107.4–15; 142.1–7
Romans 3.21–26; Romans 8.18–25; 2 Corinthians 8.1–5, 9
Mark 4.35–end; Luke 12.1–7; John 16.31–end

For the Sovereign

Joshua 1.1–9; Proverbs 8.1–16
Psalms 20; 101; 121
Romans 13.1–10; Revelation 21.22—22.4
Matthew 22.16–22; Luke 22.24–30

The anniversary of HM The King's accession is 8 September.

¶   *Psalms in the Course of a Month*

The following provision may be used for a monthly cycle of psalmody in place of the psalms provided in the tables in this booklet. It is based on the provision in The Book of Common Prayer.

	Morning Prayer	**Evening Prayer**
1	1—5	6—8
2	9—11	12—14
3	15—17	18
4	19—21	22—23
5	24—26	27—29
6	30—31	32—34
7	35—36	37
8	38—40	41—43
9	44—46	47—49
10	50—52	53—55
11	56—58	59—61
12	62—64	65—67
13	68	69—70
14	71—72	73—74
15	75—77	78
16	79—81	82—85
17	86—88	89
18	90—92	93—94
19	95—97	98—101
20	102—103	104
21	105	106
22	107	108—109
23	110—112	113—115
24	116—118	119.1–32
25	119.33–72	119.73–96
26	119.97–144	119.145–176
27	120—125	126—131
28	132—135	136—138
29	139—140	141—143
30	144—146	147—150

In February the psalms are read only to the 28th or 29th day of the month.

In January, March, May, July, August, October and December, all of which have 31 days, the same psalms are read on the last day of the month (being an ordinary weekday) which were read the day before, or else the psalms of the monthly course omitted on one of the Sundays in that month.

Concise Calendar November 2024 – December 2025

Advent 2024 to the eve of Advent 2025: Year C (Daily Eucharistic Lectionary Year 1)

November 2024

Sunday		4bAdv	3bAdv	2bAdv	ChrK
Monday		4	11	18	25
Tuesday		5	12	19	26
Wednesday		6	13	20	27
Thursday		7	14	21	28
Friday	AllSs	8	15	22	29
Saturday	2	9	16	23	30

December 2024

Sunday		Adv1	Adv2	Adv3	Adv4	Chr1
Monday		2	9	16	23	30
Tuesday		3	10	17	24	31
Wednesday		4	11	18	Chr
Thursday		5	12	19	26
Friday		6	13	20	27
Saturday		7	14	21	28

January 2025

Sunday		Chr2	Bapt	Ep2	Ep3
Monday		Epiph	13	20	27
Tuesday		7	14	21	28
Wednesday	1	8	15	22	29
Thursday	2	9	16	23	30
Friday	3	10	17	24	31
Saturday	4	11	18	25	

February 2025

Sunday		Pres	4bLnt	3bLnt	2bLnt
Monday		3	10	17	24
Tuesday		4	11	18	25
Wednesday		5	12	19	26
Thursday		6	13	20	27
Friday		7	14	21	28
Saturday	1	8	15	22	

March 2025

Sunday		NbLnt	Lnt1	Lnt2	Lnt3	Lnt4
Monday		3	10	17	24	31
Tuesday		4	11	18	Ann
Wednesday		AshW	12	19	26
Thursday		6	13	20	27
Friday		7	14	21	28
Saturday	1	8	15	22	29

April 2025

Sunday		Lnt5	PmS	Est	Est2
Monday		7	14	21	28
Tuesday	1	8	15	22	29
Wednesday	2	9	16	23	30
Thursday	3	10	17	24	
Friday	4	11	18	25	
Saturday	5	12	19	26	

May 2025

Sunday		Est3	Est4	Est5	Est6
Monday		5	12	19	26
Tuesday		6	13	20	27
Wednesday		7	14	21	28
Thursday	1	8	15	22	Ascn
Friday	2	9	16	23	30
Saturday	3	10	17	24	31

June 2025

Sunday		Est7	Pent	TrS	Tr1	Tr2
Monday		2	9	16	23	30
Tuesday		3	10	17	24
Wednesday		4	11	18	25
Thursday		5	12	19	26
Friday		6	13	20	27
Saturday		7	14	21	28

July 2025

Sunday		Tr3	Tr4	Tr5	Tr6
Monday		7	14	21	28
Tuesday	1	8	15	22	29
Wednesday	2	9	16	23	30
Thursday	3	10	17	24	31
Friday	4	11	18	25	
Saturday	5	12	19	26	

August 2025

Sunday		Tr7	Tr8	Tr9	Tr10	Tr11
Monday		4	11	18	25
Tuesday		5	12	19	26
Wednesday		6	13	20	27
Thursday		7	14	21	28
Friday	1	8	15	22	29
Saturday	2	9	16	23	30

September 2025

Sunday		Tr12	Tr13	Tr14	Tr15
Monday	1	8	15	22	29
Tuesday	2	9	16	23	30
Wednesday	3	10	17	24	
Thursday	4	11	18	25	
Friday	5	12	19	26	
Saturday	6	13	20	27	

October 2025

Sunday		Tr16	Tr17	Tr18	LstTr
Monday		6	13	20	27
Tuesday		7	14	21	28
Wednesday	1	8	15	22	29
Thursday	2	9	16	23	30
Friday	3	10	17	24	31
Saturday	4	11	18	25	

November 2025

Sunday		4bAdv	3bAdv	2bAdv	ChrK	Adv1
Monday		3	10	17	24
Tuesday		4	11	18	25
Wednesday		5	12	19	26
Thursday		6	13	20	27
Friday		7	14	21	28
Saturday	AllSs	8	15	22	29

December 2025

Sunday		Adv2	Adv3	Adv4	Chr1
Monday	1	8	15	22	29
Tuesday	2	9	16	23	30
Wednesday	3	10	17	24	31
Thursday	4	11	18	Chr	
Friday	5	12	19	26	
Saturday	6	13	20	27	

On Sunday 5 January The Epiphany of Our Lord may be celebrated, transferred from 6 January.

On Sunday 2 November All Saints' Day may be celebrated, transferred from 1 November.